Looking Back at Lincoln, Montana

"Bridge over the Blackfoot" by Nina Baril

A Scrapbook Collection about

Lincoln's Historical Places,

It's Wonderful People,

Festive Parties and

Recipes for Sweets and Treats

from

the 1950s to 1960s era

By

Karleen Hammer Anderson

ISBN 13: 978-1-59152-170-9

Published by Karleen Anderson

For more information, write
Karleen Anderson
P.O. Box 9656,
Helena, Montana 59604

You may order extra copies of this book by calling Farcountry Press toll free at (800) 821-3874.

Produced by Sweetgrass Books.
PO Box 5630, Helena, MT 59604;
(800) 821-3874;
www.sweetgrassbooks.com.

Created, produced, and designed in the United States.
Printed in the United States of America.

20 19 18 17 16 1 2 3 4 5

TABLE OF CONTENTS

A Good time for Party Foods

Winter Season Cross Stitch Design by Sandra Cozzolino

Sweets and Treats

Foreword and Dedication

What a pleasant surprise to find this advertisement for the *Betty Crocker Cookbook* in my mail one day. I have been using my grandmother's 1950s first addition for as long as I can remember. Whenever I use her old cookbook it brings back memories of baking with her in her warm and clean kitchen. It also helps me recall my father, who built her house and all the beautiful cabinets in her kitchen and sewing room. My sister and I loved to stay with our grandparents when we were small. Grandma would not only help us bake and sew, but she would save up all her catalogs and let us cut them up for paper dolls. Looking back, cutting up catalogs for paper dolls and furniture for our paper doll houses was an excellent way to keep us occupied for hours on end. What we didn't realize was that we were also learning a bit about furniture arranging and home decorating in the process.

Cooking, sewing, quilting, scrapbooking and homemaking are creative forms of artwork that are back in style. Unlike sewing or quilting, cooking doesn't leave a tangible gift or legacy to pass down from generation to generation—other than the extra pounds that collect over the years as a result of eating the fruits of our labors. I find that cookbooks are also a form of artwork that can make wonderful gifts and are also a way of preserving memories, especially if we know some of the people whose favorite recipes are featured in the cookbook.

Cookbooks and cookware by Paula Dean and Rachael Ray are now the newest rage in good cooking. Whenever I see Paula's healthy face with her glowing eyes and beautiful smile on the front page of a magazine or cookbook, I can't help but be reminded of my close friend and "second mother" June Petek. June Petek was a woman who will long be remembered and loved by all who knew her. She was a strong foundation in the formation of Lincoln, Montana's heritage during the 1950s when she and her family lived there.

In 2008, when June found out she had a short time to live, she began contacting her old friends that she had stayed in touch with over the years. With the help of her daughter Connie, she graciously wrote good-bye letters and shared some of her memories. As I tried to write back to her about my memories of her and how she influenced our lives, my letter just kept getting longer and longer. I told her about my many wonderful memories of her and so many other Lincoln women that were her friends. I also told her that I was having a brainstorm about writing some kind of a history/cookbook to let others know how her life had impacted so many people. I didn't realize as I wrote seeking permission to write something about her, how close she was to death.

In fact, she died shortly after I mailed the letter. After her death and funeral, I got a beautiful letter back from her daughter Cathie. Cathie enclosed some of June's drawings and recipes for my project. Therefore, the main reason for writing this historical type of cookbook is to honor the memory of June Petek and keep her spirit alive for many years to come. I know her family knows how precious she was to them, but will they ever know how precious she was to so many others? They may never know how many lives she helped to shape with her joy and love for life and others.

A second reason for writing this cookbook is to share my memories of some of Lincoln's other great cooks and talented homemakers from that 1950s and 1960s era. Those great ladies made Lincoln such a unique and wonderful community to live and grow up in. Most of Lincoln's great ladies were loving, kind, generous and talented homemakers who were more concerned with making life comfortable and enjoyable for others than for themselves.

In 1977, the Lincoln ladies published another of my favorite cookbooks, *The Lincoln Cookbook.* I especially enjoy the back section of the cookbook, "The Old Lincoln Cookbook," because I knew most of the ladies whose recipes were featured in that section, which must have been written before 1960. Whenever I use my favorite recipes, I can clearly recall and picture in my mind the women who wrote them. I can also recall their values and the lessons they taught me and others while we were together in Lincoln during that era.

Many of Lincoln's ladies were ambitious and hardworking women. They used their God given talents to make life enjoyable for others while making ends meet. Most of them did not have those fairy-tale marriages or picket-fenced yards and dream cottages that life is supposed to produce. Instead, most of them worked beside their husbands, helping them to support and raise their families and run a business. Lincoln women knew how to survive and continue on when a husband's death, disease, divorce, or drinking left her alone, either physically or emotionally, to face the hardships and challenges of the world by herself.

I started comparing these noble women to the "Proverbs 31" women described in the Bible. There just were not enough verses in Proverbs 31 to describe the attributes and strengths that most Lincoln women aspire to. I can't help but be reminded of Lincoln's wonderful men and women whenever I go to Lincoln or cook from my old cookbooks. Remembering my childhood with its wonderful memories of great people keeps challenging me to share their life lessons and their recipes with others.

A third reason for writing this book is to honor the memories of my own parents, Donald and Evelyn Hammer, and my sister, Donna. We were fortunate enough to live in Lincoln during our childhood years, from 1952 to 1965.

Our father, Don Hammer, was a building contractor in Lincoln until his death in 1965. At the young age of forty eight, he was kidnapped and murdered on Rogers

Pass by two men who were custom cutters hanging out in Lincoln for a few days. Why he was the one they chose as their victim, we may never know. What should be remembered about Don Hammer was his intelligence, wit and humor, work ethic and honesty. He built many of the log structures, cabins and homes around Lincoln and surrounding areas with logs that he peeled and grooved on a lathe. He designed and manufactured his lathe in his backyard garage in Great Falls. He later built a shop on Highway 200 across from the 7-Up Ranch and moved his lathe there when we moved to Lincoln around 1952. A hallmark of his logs is the 45-degree angles used for joining the corners.

Donald Hammer's biggest job in Lincoln was to build Lambkin's Bar and Cafe, which has been in use for well over fifty years. It was built during 1952 and 1953. With his building of the Lambkin's Bar and Café, he brought our little family with him to live and grow up in Lincoln.

My mother, Evelyn, was a helper and partner to my dad in his business. She was also a great homemaker, mother and cook, and helped with many community activities. Her stories and friends, along with their recipes, will be featured throughout this text. Since so many of her friends have passed on, I have to rely on her memories of them to fill in the gaps and complete their stories.

I have so enjoyed reading about Lincoln's history in the 1994 edition of *Gold Pans and Singletrees* written by several of Lincoln's citizens. The book was dedicated to Bob and Evelyn Didriksen for all their hard work and research for the history book and their help in establishing the Lincoln Historical Society. My mother was upset about our family not being represented in the book, although there are a few references about Don Hammer, such as building on the Fisher cabin and working with George Anderson.

Once when I was visiting with Ben Mayger about the history book, he explained that the group putting the book together couldn't agree on how to handle the tragic stories in the community, such as ours and the Milliron family. The group decided it was best to just leave those stories of tragedy alone.

Evelyn Hammer Young, June Petek, Donna and Karleen Hammer

Even though Don Hammer's death was a tragedy, his life wasn't. His life should be remembered for his service to others in the form of his carpentry skills, as a loving husband and father and as a friend to so many of Lincoln's citizens. Stories about him and his life would not be complete without pictures of the many beautiful and quality crafted homes in the area that he built. Most of the structures he built back in the 1950s are still in good shape and are very functional even after fifty plus years of use.

Therefore, stories about my family, the Peteks and many others who contributed to my life and Lincoln's history, along with their recipes, are featured in this volume and upcoming volumes of this cookbook, which are:

1. Party Foods and Treats
2. Bake Sales, Brides, Breads and Bazaars
3. Fruits and Vegetables and How to Pack Them in Jars
4. Fish and Game and Other Meats
5. Odds and "the End" and a Few More Sweets

Other contributions to the cookbook came in the form of artwork by several local artists to help portray the essence of growing up in Lincoln. Cartoon characters drawn by June Petek were submitted by her daughters, Connie and Cathie, along with some of their family recipes.

My favorite oil painting by Nina Baril Hiatt is of Lambkin's of Lincoln Bar and Café and is used throughout the book. A special thanks to her for allowing her daughter and son-in-law, Erin and Roger Dey, to take the photo from its home in the restaurant at Lambkin's to be photographed and printed so I could reproduce it in this publication. Thanks also to the Deys for allowing me to use several of their articles from the *Blackfoot Valley Dispatch (BVD)* for my scrapbooking.

Watercolor paintings by friend, pastor and local Helena artist Jim Howard are featured in some sections of the book. My sister, Donna Koss, also has water color paintings and drawings of some of the older homes that were built before the 1950s and 1960s era, and oil paintings of cabins and wildlife.

Photographs from my personal collections and 35mm slides that were taken by my parents are used throughout the book. Many other photographs were loaned to me for use in this book. I used newspaper articles from my scrapbook collection, along with cards, some old, some new, and several vintage and I obtained permission to use those that were copyrighted. I also used letters and pictures I have saved over many years.

Many wilderness and wildlife photographs by photographer and high school friend, Gus Wolfe, are also featured in various sections of this book.

Many food photos were taken from *Betty Crocker's Picture Cookbook* and *Wilton's Cake Decorating Yearbooks*.

I have obtained a variety of photographs from copyright free and public domain internet sites to help portray the essence of Lincoln such as snowmen, winter and Christmas scenes, table settings, flower arrangements, paper dolls and Holly Hobby dolls by Sarah Kaye.

Another favorite oil painting of mine is the old Lincoln town site by Robert Morgan, which is used in various sections of the book, along with some of his other paintings that are featured in his autobiography *My Life, My Montana* by Robert Morgan and Norma Ashby. Norma Ashby also provided photographs and editing assistance for some sections of my book. Along with Norma, I had help with editing by my sister Donna, Cathie Petek Beard, Connie Petek Hendrix, Bob McClure, Diana Welch Colton, Mary Grosfield Sampsen, and Susan Howsman, former editor of the BVD. Thanks also to Kathy Springmeyer and Shirley Machonis of Farcountry Press and Sweetgass Books for help with editing and publication.

My mother, Evelyn, provided many great stories, recipes and memories along with helping me to create and sew notebook covers, which are similar to the Bible covers she has made for so many friends and family over the years. References for recipes and articles were provided as best I could.

I obtained much information from the Lincoln history book *Gold Pans and Singletrees* along with photographs and stories from other published works which are cited within the text.

Wintertime in Lincoln, Montana

Can be a time to stay warm and cozy by a wood stove

"Bridge over the Blackfoot" by Nina Baril

Or a time to "hit the road"

for fun and frolic in the great outdoors

Wintertime in Lincoln, Montana

Can be quiet, peaceful and relaxing

Or it can be — — Partytime

Cookies from *Betty Crocker's Picture Cookbook*, First Edition (1950)

Drawing by June Petek

I have many great memories of my early childhood growing up in Lincoln, Montana. The 1950s to 1960s era was a fun time not only for growing children but for adults as well. I often think what it would be like to be able to go back to that time. Back then Lincoln was not only an isolated, beautiful little logging community, but also a community filled with loving, caring and hardworking people. I still think of those early experiences with those people and how they shaped not only my life, but the lives of many of my friends as well.

STONER'S • GENERAL • STORE
AND GARAGE
"IT PLEASES US TO PLEASE YOU"
• SEE US FOR •
GROCERIES, DRUGS, FOUNTAIN - LUNCH,
TEXACO SERVICE, FISHING SUPPLIES,
STAGE LINE, PROPANE, HARDWARE, AND
SUNDRIES
PROPS:- June and Johnny Petek
AS SKIPPER, OUR PARAKEET,
SAYS, "SHOP AT STONER'S"

Stoner's Store was the hot spot in the 1950s. The bright star in the store, and in our little town

of Lincoln, was June Petek. One of my first and fondest memories is of June working at Stoner's Store behind the lunch counter. (Stoner's Store was located on the corner of Stemple Pass Road and B Street on the now empty lot next to where the fire department is located.) I thought June Petek was about the most beautiful lady I had ever seen, except for my mother, of course. June was feminine, graceful, intelligent, energetic, talented and witty. She and her husband, John, ran the store, gas station, a propane delivery service and the Lincoln Stage.

Connie and Cathie Petek with cousins Rosalie and Dan

Birthday parties back then were a big event for kids to get together and have a good time. June's parties for her daughters, Connie and Cathie, came with balloons, decorations, fancy sandwiches, treats, cake, ice cream, games with prizes and, best of all, presents. There was much fun and laughter, and June made everyone feel like they were special and a part of her family. Her little house on the back of the store was so cute, cozy and inviting for anyone to come to.

Whether June was cooking at the lunch counter or making treats for a bunch of kids, her cooking was the greatest. I have cherished a cookbook that June gave me for one of my childhood birthdays. The cookbook, *Better Homes and Gardens Junior Cookbook for the Hostess and Host of Tomorrow* (1955), was a great way to learn to cook. I used it to help teach my daughters to cook as well. I will reference this cookbook for some of the recipes I use often and also for the party sandwiches on the next page.

Proverbs 31: 10-12 "If you can find a truly good wife, she is worth more than precious gems! Her husband can trust her, and she will richly satisfy his needs. She will not hinder him, but help him all her life."

<u>Party Surprise Sandwiches</u>
2 (3 oz.) packages cream cheese
¼ cup milk
1 (5 oz.) can boned chicken
2 tbsp. mayonnaise
1 (5 oz.) jar pimiento-cheese spread
12 stuffed olives, chopped
18 slices bread, crusts removed
Soft margarine or butter

Soften cream cheese. Stir in milk gradually. Beat smooth each time you add milk.
Cut chicken into small pieces. Put in another bowl; add mayonnaise.
Put the cheese spread in a third bowl and stir in the chopped olives.
Butter bread. Spread with chicken mixture; add slice of bread. Spread with cheese; top with third slice of bread. Frost with softened cream cheese. Decorate top with olives, if desired. Chill. Sandwich can be carefully cut into 3 or 4 slices for a small ribbon sandwich, if desired.

<u>Tea-Party Sandwiches</u>

Better Homes and Garden Jr. Cookbook

Ingredients:

Bread, white or whole grain-With an open topped deep cookie cutter, cut out 2 pieces of bread the same shape for each sandwich you will make. Make into stars, hearts, bells, triangles or whatever shape fits the occasion.

Butter, softened -Spread a cut out with butter. Be sure to get it out to the edge.

Egg salad, tuna salad, chicken salad, salmon salad, beef spread or cucumber and cream cheese mixture can be spread on one piece of bread before topping with the second slice of a cut out bread shape.

A third piece of bread and another filling can be added to make a ribbon sandwich as described in the above recipe.

<u>Salmon Salad Sandwich Filling</u>
1 (7 oz.) can flaked salmon (*I use Costco's Kirkland brand; I found a certain discount store's brand to be nothing but skin, fins, bones and eyeballs–just kidding)*
¼ cup chopped celery
¼ cup chopped onion
1 to 2 Tbsp. salad dressing
½ tsp. dill weed

Chop salmon in a bowl. Add all the other ingredients and mix well. Chill. Serve as a salad with tomatoes and crackers or use as a sandwich filling.

<u>Left-Over Roast Beef Sandwich Spread</u> (*my mother's specialty and my favorite*)

2 cups ground cooked leftover roast beef
⅓ cup sweet relish or sweet pickle, chopped
½ tsp. salt
⅓ cup chopped onion
1 cup salad dressing

Mix altogether. Chill. Spread on bread for sandwich or use for ribbon sandwich with another slice of bread and cucumber spread. (See page 19)

Stoner's Store was the Peteks family home for several years. There was a doorway to the house from the store that was close to the lunch counter. June could keep an eye on her two young daughters whether they were in the store with her or in the house. The picture of Cathie and Connie growing up at the store is so cute. Note: How about the sign in the background that says "sugar 10# - 1.00."

Cathie and Connie Petek in Stoner's Store about 1950

June also had a first-aid station in the store for those who needed a little patching up from minor traumas. June, with her first aid-kit, was the only source of medical help in our town until Dr. Elmer Smith arrived in 1957 and Vernie Burns, RN, soon after.

June taught first-aid classes to our Girl Scout Troop one winter. We would either meet in her home at the back of the store or the Lincoln Community Hall. We had a lot of fun learning the basic skills of first aid, which for some of us became an introduction to the world of medical care.

June Petek with Connie and Cathie

Our Girl Scout troop loved having June as our leader. She would let us use her kitchen and helped us learn how to bake and cook. I don't know how she tolerated the messes that we made there. She was always patient with us though. With her sense of humor and her jolly nature, she just took it all in stride.

June's kitchen at the back of Stoner's Store saw a lot of other activities. June baked and decorated fancy cakes and cookies for bake sales and school functions.

One activity that was our Girl Scout troop's big moneymaker was the sale of apple fritters fresh out of the fryer. My mother would help her with that sale, which was not an easy task. Mom and June would be preparing and deep fat frying apple fritters as fast as they could to keep up with our Girl Scout delivery service. We would take orders before the big day, and then pedal our bikes as fast as possible to get the fritters to our customers while they were still hot. The back door to June's kitchen just kept swinging open and shut as girls entered to get their orders filled. Our customers would be waiting at their doors with their forks and money in hand. The fritters were always a big hit, and a good time was had by all.

Apple Fritters

by June and Evelyn from
Betty Crocker's Cookbook

2 eggs
½ cups milk
1 cup sifted flour
1 tsp. baking powder
1 tsp. salt
1 tsp. vegetable oil
1 to 2 cups cut up apple slices
Hot fat for deep fat frying

Beat the eggs. Stir in milk. Sift flour, baking powder and salt together and stir in. Beat in the oil. Add cup up fruit (apples or bananas). Drop by spoonfuls into hot deep fat and fry at 375 degrees until brown. Drain and serve hot with syrup.

Corn Fritters

Follow recipe above – adding **1 cup grated-off-the-cob cooked corn or drained canned whole kernel corn** to fritter batter. Drop by spoonfuls into hot fat.

French Donuts

Evelyn Hammer Young

1 cup water
¼ cup butter
¼ tsp. salt
2 Tbsp. sugar
1¼ cups sifted flour
4 eggs
1 tsp. vanilla extract
Hot fat for deep fat frying

1. Cut out 14 (3 inch) foil circles. Grease one side well
2. Bring water, butter, salt and sugar to a boil in a 2½ quart saucepan.
3. Add flour all at once and stir until mixture forms a smooth ball. Cool.
4. Add eggs, one at a time, beating well after addition of each egg. Add vanilla and beat until mixture is shiny.
5. Turn into a pastry bag using #6 star tube and press onto foil circles. Let stand 20 minutes before frying in 365 degree oil. Foil will separate while cooking. Remove foil from pan and fry donuts for 7 minutes. Turn frequently. Drain.
6. Dust with powdered sugar or glaze.

Orange Butter Glaze

1¾ cup powdered sugar
2 Tbsp. orange juice
2 tsp. grated orange peel
3 Tbsp. butter

Combine all ingredients and put on donuts while still warm.

Sour Cream Doughnuts

Vernie Burns
Old Lincoln Cookbook

5 eggs
2 cups sugar
1 cup thick sour cream
2 cups buttermilk
Hot fat for frying
8 cups flour
2 tsp. baking powder
1 tsp. soda
vanilla or nutmeg for flavoring

Beat eggs. Add sugar and sour cream. Sift flour, baking powder and salt. Add the dry ingredients alternately with the buttermilk. Chill before rolling. Fry in deep fat fryer at 365 degrees until brown. Dust with powdered sugar or glaze (see above) or serve plain.

The Lincoln Cookbook

Another of my favorite cookbooks is *The Lincoln Cookbook* written by the Pine Grove Extension Homemakers in 1977. It is white with a green binding, and on the cover is a drawing by Jerry Burns of bears after honey. Mrs. Deanne Moffitt gave a copy to me as a Christmas present that year. I have tried many of the great recipes, but find that my favorite recipes are in the "Old Lincoln Cookbook" section at the very end.

It is my favorite section because I knew and still remember most of the women who wrote those recipes, seeing their faces and recalling memories of them each time I cook one of their recipes. Several of their recipes are included throughout the various sections of this book.

I still remember the original Home Extension group and how much fun those women had at their meetings. They took turns each month hosting a luncheon and demonstration.

My mother learned a great deal of homemaking and decorating skills at those meetings. There was just one problem—my mother would panic each time it was her turn to host a party. I would find this a great time to skip school for the day so as to help her get ready. When the ladies arrived, I would play sick, but loved to listen in on what they were learning.

Pat Sias was the Home Extension agent from Helena who helped establish the group and taught new methods for cooking, crafting, homemaking and budgeting. That eager group of women had a goal to be the best wives, mothers and homemakers they could be, and they took that job seriously.

My Dad would refer to the Home Extension meetings as "hen parties." Although he was just referring to all the noise and laughter, I do recall egg and chicken dishes were always a hit. Maybe it was an appropriate name after all. Since eggs are always an enjoyable and easy-to-prepare food for parties and brunches, I have included several recipes for egg dishes on the next few pages.

Cucumber Spread

1 large package cream cheese
1 cucumber, finally chopped
Mix together and spread on bread.

Egg Salad sandwich filling

Cook **8 eggs** in hot water for 12 minutes. Peel eggs while still warm; chill. Chop the eggs into a bowl.
Add:
4 Tbsp. celery, chopped fine
4 Tbsp. salad dressing
2 tsp. green onion, chopped
2 tsp. prepared mustard
½ tsp. salt Dash pepper
Mix together. Keep refrigerated until ready to use.

Stuffed Eggs

Cook the eggs as previously directed. Cut the eggs in half lengthwise. Remove the yolks and put them in a small bowl. Put the whites aside. Mash the yolks and stir in:

2 Tbsp. mayonnaise
1 tsp. vinegar
1 tsp. prepared mustard
¼ tsp. paprika
½ tsp. salt
Dash pepper

Stir until smooth. Spoon egg mixture into whites. Arrange on a plate with parsley. Sprinkle with paprika.

Tuna Salad for sandwich or Tomato Royal
2 cans drained tuna (about 1 cup)
½ cup minced celery
1 tbsp. sweet pickle relish
1 egg, hard boiled
¼ cup salad dressing
1 tsp. minced onion, opt.
Mash egg, add and combine all other ingredients in a bowl; chill.

Tomato Royal
Cut each **tomato** (need 4 to 6) into 6 sections, almost to stem end; place each tomato on a **bed of lettuce** on a luncheon plate; fill with a chilled salad filling, such as tuna (see above recipe), salmon salad or chicken salad (below)

Calcutta Chicken or Turkey Salad
2 cups cooked turkey or chicken, chopped
1 (10 oz.) can mandarin orange segments, drained
½ cup salad dressing or blue cheese salad dressing
½ cup green pepper, chopped
½ cup celery, chopped
½ tsp. curry powder

Combine all chopped ingredients. Add dressing and curry powder; toss lightly.

Another favorite childhood cookbook was Mary Ald
Cookbook for Children. This book was a gift from my mot
in 1956. It has been so well used by myself and my childr
that the pages are tattered, well-worn and disintegrating.

ARY ALDEN'S COOK BOOK FOR CHILDRE
64 PAGES OF SIMPLE RECIPES

LE PAGE)

FRIED EGG MORNING
(MAKES 1 SERVING)

THE FOOD YOU NEED

THE TOOLS YOU NEED

WHAT TO DO

1. MELT BUTTER SLOWLY
2. BREAK INTO CUP CAREFULLY
3. NOW PUT IN PAN CAREFULLY
4. KEEP SPOONING BUTTER OVER TILL WHITE IS VERY WHITE

SPRINKLE WITH SALT AND PEPPER

Published by WONDER BOOKS, Inc.
1107 Broadway New York, N. Y.

Farmhouse Omelets
(makes two omelets)

4 bacon strips, diced
¼ cup chopped onion
Dash hot pepper sauce
3 tsp. butter, divided
½ cup cubed fully cooked ham, *divided*
¼ cup thinly sliced fresh mushrooms, *divided*
¼ cup chopped green pepper, *divided*
1 cup (4 oz.) shredded cheddar cheese, *divided*
6 eggs
¼ tsp. salt, optional
1 Tbsp. water
⅛ tsp. pepper

In a skillet, cook bacon over medium heat until crisp. Remove with a slotted spoon to paper towels. Drain, reserving 2 tsp. drippings. In the drippings, saute onion until tender; set aside. In a bowl, beat eggs, water, salt if desired, pepper and hot pepper sauce. Melt 1½ teaspoons butter in a 10-inch nonstick skillet over medium heat; add half of the egg mixture. As the eggs set, lift edges, letting uncooked portion flow underneath.

When eggs are set, sprinkle half of the bacon, onion, ham, mushrooms, green pepper and cheese over one side; fold over. Cover and let stand 1 to 2 minutes or until cheese is melted. Repeat with remaining ingredients for second omelet.

always crack eggs in a separate bowl before adding them to your concoction

Chicken and Broccoli Braid

2 cups cooked chicken, chopped
½ cup red bell pepper, chopped
4 oz. sharp cheddar cheese, shredded (1 cup)
¼ tsp. salt
2 pkgs. (8 oz. each) refrigerated crescent rolls
1 cup broccoli, chopped
1 garlic clove, pressed
½ cup mayonnaise
2 tsp. dried dill weed
1 egg white, slightly beaten
2 Tbsp. slivered almonds

Preheat oven to 375 degrees. Chop chicken, broccoli and bell pepper and place in a bowl. Press garlic over vegetable mixture. Shred cheese and add to vegetable mixture; mix gently. Add mayonnaise, dill and salt; mix well.

Unroll one package of crescent dough; do not separate. Arrange longest sides of dough across width of 12 x 15-rectangle baking stone or pan. Repeat with remaining package of dough. Using a pizza roller, roll dough to seal perforations. On longest sides of baking stone or pan, cut dough into strips 1½ inches apart, 3 inches deep. (There will be 6 inches in the center for the filling.)

Spread filling evenly over middle of dough. To braid, lift strips of dough across mixture to meet in center, twisting each strip one turn. Continue alternating strips to form a braid. Tuck ends up to seal at end of braid.

Brush egg white over dough with a pastry brush. Sprinkle with almonds. Bake 25 to 28 minutes or until deep golden brown. Cut and serve. Yields 10 servings.

Curly Pasta and Chicken Toss

1 pkg. (8 oz.) uncooked fusilli pasta or spaghetti
1 can (10½ oz.) condensed chicken broth
2 large carrots
1 pound boneless, skinless chicken breast halves
2 tsp. vegetable oil, divided
2 cups broccoli flowerets
1 oz. fresh Parmesan cheese, grated (¼ cup)
2 Tbsp. cornstarch
½ tsp. salt
1 medium bell pepper
1 lemon
2 garlic cloves, pressed
2 Tbsp. fresh snipped or dried basil leaves

Cook pasta according to package directions. Drain and keep warm. Meanwhile, combine cornstarch and salt in a 1 qt. bowl. Whisk in chicken broth; set aside. Zest lemon and add to chicken broth mixture. Cut carrots diagonally into ¼ inch thick slices. Cut pepper into 1 inch pieces. Cut chicken into 1 inch strips. Heat 1 tsp. of the oil over medium-high heat in stir-fry skillet until hot. Press garlic into skillet. Add chicken; stir-fry for 5 minutes. Remove from skillet. Heat remaining 1 tsp. oil in skillet; add carrots and stir-fry 2 minutes. Add broccoli and bell pepper; stir-fry 2-3 minutes until vegetables are crisp-tender. Add broth mixture and browned chicken. Bring to a boil; reduce heat to medium and cook until mixture is slightly thickened, stirring occasionally. Remove from heat. Stir in fusilli and basil. Serve immediately. Grate Parmesan cheese over pasta. Top with pepper, if desired.

Jean Bossing was another of my favorite mentors from the past and another example of a Proverbs 31 woman. She and her husband, Bob, moved to Lincoln from back East. They were both well educated--Jean was a nurse, and Bob had been a college professor. Bob had trouble finding work that fit his qualifications and level of education in Lincoln. Jean was very ambitious and thrifty. She soon put her talents to work to help make ends meet as they struggled to adapt to the western ways. Jean taught piano lessons in the home they rented from the Grosfields. I loved to ride my bike to her house for my lessons. I remember it being a big two-story, log house with the kitchen and entryway built on the south side. It had a pond with a small stream running through it, with some old buildings and corrals around the area. It was in a clearing with a great view of the mountains to the north.

I have often wondered if that house was still standing after all these years. Every time I tried to find it, the gate was locked on the road off Sucker Creek. The only other way to it was to go north on Airport Road, which used to go past it and meet up with another road that connected to Sucker Creek Road. Any time we tried to approach from that route, we ended up in somebody's yard. Things change and roadways disappear after fifty years.

I had begun to think this house and the memories that went with it were all a figment of my imagination. I know my husband thought we were just out on a wild goose chase every time we tried to find it. Then one day, we drove up Sucker Creek Road about half a mile and off to the right and across from the old Mayger place, there was my first break in the case. *The gate was open*! My husband protested as I made him turn into the lane. He said since there was now a mailbox out along the road that showed somebody lived there, we were trespassing.
I told him I just had to take that road to prove to him that I wasn't crazy, and reminded him that this wouldn't be his first time trespassing. As we drove down that road, everything was as I remembered it until we got to a house. Then the road turned into a trail just past the turn into the house. My husband said, "This is the end of the road, what do you plan on doing now?" I told him to follow that narrow little road because it was just around the bend. For once he did as I suggested and there it was—just as I had remembered it.

The pond, the view, the *small* two-story log house, and even signs of a road running south to west that would have joined up with Airport Road and Sucker Creek Road many years in the past. It was sad to see this lonely little house that looked like nobody had lived there, except for little critters, for many, many years. *Proverbs 31: 17 and 18 "She is energetic, a hard worker, and watches for bargains. She works far into the night!"*

The original homestead house of Matthew King, built in the 1880s, is the oldest remaining building in the Lincoln area. It is built of hand-hewn, square logs about 20 inches in diameter. The original 720-acre King Homestead was purchased in 1947 by the Grosfields. (*Gold Pans and Singletrees*, 1994)

Make sure to also feed our feathered Friends

Chicken Grape Salad

Evelyn Hammer Young

2 cups cut up cold cooked chicken, large chunks
1 cup ½ inch cut up celery
1 cup sweet green grapes, halved
Salt and pepper to taste
½ cup mayonnaise, thinned with 1 Tbsp. lemon juice
½ cup salted almonds

Mix all ingredients together. Keep chilled until ready to serve.

Chicken or Tuna Roll-Ups

Maxine Skaw
Old Lincoln Cookbook

Crust: Sift together: **2 cups flour, 3 tsp. baking powder and 1 tsp. salt**
Pour into a cup: **⅓ cup vegetable oil and ⅔ cup milk,** but do not stir. Pour all at once into flour and stir dough with a fork until mixture cleans from sides of bowl. Knead dough 10 times. Roll dough on a floured board until ¼ inch thick. Cut into squares and spread with 2 tablespoons filling and roll up.
Filling: **1 (7 oz.) can chicken or tuna, 1 unbeaten egg, and ½ cup celery, diced, ¼ cup chopped onion, if desired.** Place sealed side down on ungreased cookie sheet. Bake 10 to 15 minutes at 450 degrees. Serve hot with **heated, undiluted cream of celery or mushroom soup** poured over top of roll-ups.

Make Ahead Eggs Benedict

Cathie Petek Beard

4 English muffins, split and toasted
16 thin slices Canadian-style bacon or ham
¼ cup all-purpose flour
⅛ tsp. each ground nutmeg and pepper
2 cups shredded Swiss cheese
½ cup crushed cornflakes (about 1 cup before crushing)
8 eggs
¼ cup butter
1 tsp. paprika
2 cups milk
½ cup dry white wine
1 Tbsp. butter, melted

In a 9 x 13-inch baking dish arrange muffins, cut side up. Place 2 bacon or ham slices on each muffin half. Half fill 10-inch skillet with water; bring just to boiling. Break one egg into a dish. Carefully slide egg into water. Repeat with three more eggs. Simmer uncovered, 3 minutes until just set. Remove eggs with a slotted spoon. Repeat with remaining eggs. Place one egg on top of each muffin stack.
Sauce: In a medium size saucepan, melt ¼ cup butter, stir in flour, paprika, nutmeg and pepper. Add milk all at once. Cook and stir until thickened and bubbly. Stir in cheese till it melts. Stir in wine. Spoon sauce over muffin stacks. Combine cornflakes and butter, sprinkle over muffin stacks. Cover; chill overnight.
To serve: Bake,uncovered in a 375 degree oven, 20-25 min. or until heated through.

Photo of Randy & Connie (Petek) Hendrix in 2012 on another trespassing adventure to the old Matt King house, owned by the Grosfields and rented by the Bossings in the 1950-1960 era.

Creamed Eggs (hard cooked eggs, cut into quarters) with whites and some of yolks in a White Sauce, poured over buttered toast or biscuits with sieved yolks over the top.

Picture from Betty Crocker's Picture Cookbook First Edition (1950)

Individual Breakfast Cups

3 cups frozen potatoes O'Brien
1 cup diced ham
4 large eggs
2 cups shredded Cheddar cheese, divided
¾ cup evaporated milk

Prepare potatoes according to package skillet directions, salt and pepper to taste. Stir in ham and 1 cup cheese. Divide among 1 (12 count) muffin pan. In medium bowl, combine milk and eggs; salt and pepper to taste. Whisk until well combined. Pour over potatoes. Top with remaining cheese. Bake in a preheated, 350 degree oven, 20 minutes or until eggs are set.

Mushroom Zucchini Frittata

1 large onion, chopped
1 cup thinly sliced fresh mushrooms
⅓ cup milk
½ tsp. ground mustard
1 cup (4 oz.) shredded Swiss cheese
2 medium zucchini, halved and thinly sliced
4½ tsps. butter
1 tsp. Dijon mustard
3 eggs
¼ tsp. pepper
¼ tsp. salt
2 Tbsp. dry bread crumbs

In a large skillet, sauté the onion, zucchini and mushrooms in butter until tender; drain. Transfer to an 8-inch square baking dish coated with cooking spray. In a large bowl, whisk the eggs, milk, mustards, salt and pepper; pour over vegetable mixture. Sprinkle with cheese and bread crumbs.
Bake, uncovered, at 375 degrees for 18 to 22 minutes or until set. Let stand for 5 minutes.

Eggs with Savory Sauce

Eleanor Wing/Vernie Burns' sister-in-law
Old Lincoln Cookbook

Place shelled **hard-cooked, cut-in-half eggs** in oiled baking pan. Sauté **2 tsp. minced onion, ¼ cup diced green pepper in ¼ cup butter** until soft. Mix **pinch of thyme, ½ cup non-fat dry milk, ½ cup flour, 1 tsp. salt, ½ tsp. paprika.** Stirring constantly, add **2 cups water** and cook until sauce is thickened. Pour over egg halves and bake 15 minutes at 400 degrees.

Wisconsin Brunch Bake

4 cups cooked corn bread, coarsely crumbled
1 cup cheddar cheese, shredded
¼ cup onion, finely chopped
2 cups milk
¾ tsp. Worcestershire sauce, divided
2 cups cooked ham, diced
⅓ cup green pepper, chopped
1 (4 oz.) can sliced mushrooms
4 eggs, beaten
2 Tbsp. butter, melted

Heat oven to 350 degrees. Lightly grease a 9 x 13-inch baking dish. In a large bowl, combine 3¼ cups crumbled corn bread, ham, cheese, green pepper, onions and mushrooms. Mix well. Combine milk, eggs, and ½ tsp. Worcestershire sauce; add to corn bread mixture, mixing well. Pour into baking dish. Combine remaining ¾ cup crumbled corn bread, butter and ¼ tsp. remaining Worcestershire sauce; mix well. Sprinkle over top of casserole. Bake uncovered about 45 minutes until set.

Smoked Sausage Strata

6 smoked sausage, casing removed, chopped
6 slices white bread, cut into ½ inch cubes
6 eggs
2 cups milk
⅛ tsp. celery salt
1 cup fresh mushrooms, sliced
2 cups sharp cheddar cheese, shredded
1 tsp. dry mustard
1 tsp. dried oregano flakes

Butter a 9x13- inch baking dish. Scatter bread cubes on bottom. Top with sausage, bacon, or ham. Spread cheese over all. Beat the milk and eggs together. Add seasonings and mix well. Pour over sausage mixture. Cover with plastic wrap and refrigerate 6 hours or overnight. Preheat oven to 325 degrees. Bake, uncovered, 40 to 45 minutes or until golden brown.

Baked Eggs

Mrs. Horsky/ *Old Lincoln Cookbook*

Break **eggs** into well-buttered muffin tins; salt lightly and cover with **thin cream.** Sprinkle with **parsley and grated cheese.** Bake in preheated oven at 350 degrees for 10 minutes or until white of egg is thickened.

Jean would sometimes have me help her with babysitting her three children and with household chores. Jean was very thrifty and was always willing to share her budgeting secrets with others. In fact, she would give me piano lessons in exchange for the help I gave her. She made the best oatmeal cookies around. I finally asked her what was her secret to making such good cookies. She said she couldn't afford shortening or butter, so she used lard instead. Back then, lard was also my mother's secret ingredient to making flaky pie crust. Even after I found out about the lard, her cookies were still one of my favorites. Jean said she also used a lot of oatmeal for cooking and breakfast, because it was cheap and filling. That's good because one would need the oatmeal and its fiber to help flush that lard (cholesterol) out of the body before it could get to the arteries and help prevent the plaque buildup that would occur.

Jean was a very talented musician who also played piano and the organ for the church. I used to get bored easily with classical music, which was Jean's specialty. Jean was very precise with counting, timing, tempo, fingering, pedaling, etc. I thought all that was a waste of my time, since I only wanted to play like Floyd Cramer, not Chopin. I hounded my Mom for so long, that she finally found me the sheet music for "Last Date." I figured I could finally stump Jean with this pop-country song since it was not her type of music.

I took the new "Last Date" sheet music to my next lesson and asked Jean if she could teach me to play it. With her perfect counting, timing, fingering, tempo, etc., she played it almost as well as good old Floyd. All she was lacking was the "slip note" style that made Floyd's country sound so distinct. She about knocked me off my piano stool as I watched and listened to her play. I gained a new appreciation for her that day. I also learned that it would take hard work, practice and commitment if I was ever going to be able to play like that.

Jean also used a lot of powdered milk for drinking and baking. As hard as I tried, I just couldn't drink that stuff. It was even worse on oatmeal or for making tapioca pudding. I have also heard that babies and small children need the fat content from whole milk for proper development and growth. Once they are old enough to eat oatmeal cookies, though, they should do just fine with powdered milk

Egg-Cheese Brunch

Butter a 9 x 13-inch pan. Line with **6 slices white bread with crusts removed.** Crumble on **2 cups crisp bacon or diced ham or sausage.** Sprinkle with **2 cups grated cheddar cheese.** Top with **¾ cup chopped green onion** (optional). Sprinkle with **salt, pepper and parsley.** Beat **1 dozen eggs** until foamy. Add **1 cup milk or sour cream.** Pour over the other ingredients. Cover and refrigerate overnight. Bake on top rack in oven at 375 degrees for about 45 minutes. Watch closely. Insert knife to check to see if done. If knife comes out clean then it's ready to serve.

Speedy Sausage Squares

1 tube (8 oz.) refrigerated crescent roll
1 pound bulk pork sausage
6 eggs, lightly beaten
¾ cup milk
2 Tbsp. green pepper, chopped
1 cup (4 oz.) mozzarella cheese, shredded
¼ cup chopped onion
¼ tsp. garlic salt
½ tsp. dried oregano
½ tsp. pepper

Unroll crescent dough into a greased 9 x 13-inch baking dish; seal seams and perforations. Bake at 375 degrees for 6 minutes or until golden brown.
Meanwhile, in a skillet, cook sausage and onion over medium heat until meat is no longer pink; drain. In a bowl, combine the eggs, milk, spices and green pepper; pour over the crust. Sprinkle with sausage mixture. Bake for 15-20 minutes. Sprinkle with cheese, bake 5 minutes longer or until cheese is melted.

Two Cheese Spinach Quiche

1 unbaked pie pastry
½ cup fresh spinach
1 can ham (5½ oz.) flaked. Can use bacon or sausage instead, if desired
3 eggs
2 Tbsp. flour
¼ cup cheddar cheese
½ cup Swiss cheese, finely chopped
½ cup fresh mushrooms, sliced
1 cup half-and-half
½ tsp. salt

Line the unbaked pastry shell with a double thickness of heavy duty foil. Bake at 450 degrees for 5 minutes. Remove the foil; bake 5 minutes longer. Reduce heat to 350 degrees. Combine Swiss cheese, spinach, mushrooms and ham. Sprinkle over the crust. In a bowl, beat eggs, cream, flour and salt until smooth. Pour over spinach mixture. Sprinkle with cheddar cheese. Bake 40-45 minutes, or until knife inserted comes out clean.
Note: If using frozen spinach, be sure to drain it well after thawing and let it dry on paper towels before using.

Deluxe Scrambled Eggs

2 oz. cream cheese
⅓ cup diced cooked ham
1 Tbsp. milk
3 eggs
1 tsp. butter or margarine
1 green onion, sliced thin

Microwave cream cheese and milk on HIGH 25-30 seconds or until softened. Add eggs; whisk until blended. In a small pan, heat butter until melted. Add ham, green onion and egg mixture. Over medium heat, cook and stir until eggs are set. Salt and pepper to taste.

Donna and Percy

I use a lot of powdered milk for baking, making breads, pancakes and hot chocolate. It is great to have on hand in the pantry for emergencies. It has sure helped me in times of power outages, floods, blizzards and short paychecks. I also use a lot of powdered milk for feeding puppies when they are being weaned from their mother and need their dry dog food moistened. They seem to do just as well on it as the very expensive dog milk replacers. I only had two dogs as a child, so I make up for it now that my children are grown and gone.

Our Manx cat, Percy, had many, many kittens while we lived in Lincoln. I am sure there are still descendants of hers running around there yet. I wonder if we used powdered milk to feed that cat and all those kittens.

As for powdered milk, there are some name brands out there that are about as expensive as buying the real thing. Remember to watch the prices and look for bargains.

While we were away at high school in Augusta and then college, Jean and Bob Bossing started raising chickens at the south end of First Avenue and C Street. Those barns are still there today and being used for some type of iron-works industry.

Jean and Bob had quite a large egg and poultry production, and Jean became known as the "egg lady." I heard that Jean stayed up late at night candling the eggs to find any imperfections before packaging them to sell. This took a toll on her health, and she suffered from a neck injury from working so hard on her egg production business. Jean lived a hard life and worked very hard to take care of her family. Moving away from her prestigious family back East and coming out West to make a new start was difficult for her, as it would be for anybody. Losing a child though, was probably her worst struggle. I don't know how she was ever able to recover from that. But with her sense of humor, faith and hard work, she tried to make the best of any situation she was in. She is another example of the Proverbs 31 woman. *Proverbs 31: 30, 31 "Charm can be deceptive and beauty doesn't last, but a woman who fears and reverences God shall be greatly praised. Praise her for the many fine things she does. These good deeds of hers shall bring her honor and recognition."*

While I was looking through *The Lincoln Cookbook,* I came upon the same Oatmeal Crispies recipe that Jean used, but it was written by Maxine Skaw. I then remembered that Jean and Maxine had been friends. I didn't know Maxine or her family back

Your Friendship Is a Treasure

Jean's Oatmeal Cookies

Jean Bossing/Maxine Skaw
Old Lincoln Cookbook

1 cup shortening
1 cup brown sugar
1 cup granulated sugar
2 well beaten eggs
1 tsp. vanilla
1½ cups flour
1 tsp. salt
1 tsp. soda
3 cups quick oatmeal
½ cup chopped nuts

Cream shortening and sugars. Beat in eggs and vanilla. Add sifted dry ingredients. Shape into rolls. Wrap in waxed paper. Chill overnight. Slice ¼ inch thick. Bake for 10 minutes on a greased cookie sheet. (I do the lazy way and just drop them by a teaspoonful on a cookie sheet and bake).

Fat Free Granola

Ann Skaw Ward

Mix until sugar dissolves:
¾ cup brown sugar
⅓ can apple juice (frozen, concentrated)
½ cup powdered milk
½ tsp. salt
1 Tbsp. cinnamon
⅓ cup honey

Add and mix in:
5 cups quick oatmeal
½ cup dried fruit
Can also add nuts, coconut etc.

Spread out on a cookie sheet and bake at 375 degrees for 20-30 minutes. Stir frequently.

Oatmeal Cake

Maxine Skaw

1¼ cup boiling water
1 cup quick oatmeal
1 stick butter or margarine (½ cup)
1 cup sugar
1 cup brown sugar
1⅓ cup flour
1 tsp. cinnamon
½ tsp. salt
1 tsp. soda
2 eggs

Stir oatmeal and margarine into water, cover and let sit 20 minutes. Then stir in all other ingredients. Bake 30 minutes in a moderate oven.

***Icing*:**
6 Tbsp. margarine
½ cup chopped nuts
¼ cup cream or canned milk
½ cup coconut
½ cup sugar
1 tsp. vanilla

Combine all ingredients and spread on cake as soon as cake comes out of the oven. Put under broiler until coconut is browned; watch very carefully.

No Bake Cookies

Karla Anderson Butcher

2 cups sugar
½ cup margarine
½ cup milk or cream
2 Tbsp. cocoa

Mix and cook for 1 full minute at a full boil. Remove from heat and add:
1 tsp. vanilla
3 cups quick oatmeal
½ cup chunky peanut butter

Drop by teaspoonfuls on waxed paper and cool.

then, as her girls were younger than my friends and I. I later got to know Maxine's daughter, Ann, quite well when we moved to Helena back in the 1980s. Ann's husband, Ron Ward, was the minister in the first church we attended when we moved to Helena from Augusta. Both Ron and Ann were gifted piano players. Ron taught my three daughters piano lessons until he and his family moved to Bozeman. Ron then became one of the pastors in a very large church there. Ron became quite disabled after a serious stroke in 1993 and died about fourteen years later. Ann helped him keep his ministry going by helping him pastor youth groups and a small church while taking an active part with his rehabilitation. Anybody who has the privilege of knowing Ann can't help but love her and admire her patience, hope and perseverance in the face of hardships.

Proverbs 31: 25, 29 "She is a woman of strength and dignity. When she speaks, her words are wise, and kindness is the rule for everything she says. Her children stand and bless her; so does her husband. He praises her with these words: There are many fine women in the world, but you are the best of them all!"

Ryan, Raelynn and Rachelle with parents Ann and Ron Ward—1996

My daughters, Karla, Lisa and Lana Anderson with pastor and music teacher Ron Ward in 1986

ana Anderson on her 13th birthday party, 1990, with the Wards—Ann, Ron and Raelynn

HAPPY BIRTHDAY!

Sweet Memories

Craft Day Molded Rainbow Salad

Jean Bossing
Lincoln Cookbook

1 small box orange Jello
1 small box pineapple Jello
1 small box lemon Jello
1 small box lime Jello
1 small box strawberry-banana Jello
2 (8 oz.) pkgs. cream cheese
Sweet cream
1 small pkg. walnuts
1 cup crushed pineapple, drained
1 jar red maraschino cherries
1 cup grapefruit sections, drained
2 small cans orange sections
2 bananas, sliced
1 pkg. frozen strawberries, thawed
2 cups celery, chopped

First Step: Prepare orange and pineapple Jello according to box, reducing water by half. Hasten thickening process by adding some ice cubes and stirring quickly. Then add pineapple and cherries. Pour into small punch bowl and chill until firm.

Second Step: Prepare lemon and lime Jello according to box, reducing water by half. Follow procedure above. Then add grapefruit and orange sections. Then add generous amount of walnuts. Add this to the punch bowl and refrigerate until slightly thickened.

Third Step: Meanwhile, mix softened cream cheese with sweet cream until of spreading consistency. Spread light layer over layer of Jello which by now is firm in punch bowl. Let set one hour.

Fourth Step: Prepare strawberry Jello according to box, reducing water by half. Follow previous procedure. Then add celery, bananas, and the strawberries (without the juice). Add this layer to the punch bowl and refrigerate until firm.

Fifth Step: With the remaining half of the cream cheese mixture, put the final layer on the very top and sprinkle some chopped walnuts on for garnish.

This recipe makes enough for a small punch bowl and is very pretty served from the bowl.

11 Layer Rainbow Jello Squares

6 packages Jello (3 oz. each) of strawberry, orange, lemon, lime, blue raspberry and grape. (Choose any flavors you wish. This recipe is based on colors)
8½ envelopes KNOX unflavored gelatin
1 (14 oz.) can sweetened condensed milk

Mix the can of condensed milk with 1¾ cups hot water. (Microwave for 3 minutes to get water to boil). Set aside. Mix 2½ envelopes KNOX gelatin with 1¼ cups hot water and combine with the milk mixture and set aside.

Combine grape Jello, 1 envelope KNOX gelatin with 1¼ cups hot water. Stir to dissolve. Cool, and then pour into a 9 x 13-inch Pyrex and a 10 x10-inch Pyrex square baking dish. Place in the freezer for 15 minutes or until firm.

Now would be a great time to get your next layer (blue raspberry) ready so that it will be cool enough to pour over grape layer when it is ready. Pour a thin layer of the milk mixture on top of the grape Jello then freeze to set. Next pour the blue layer and then prepare the green layer. Pour milk over the blue layer . . . followed by preparing the green layer while preparing the yellow layer. Repeat, you get the idea . . . Continue until you get to the last layer, the red layer.

Note: If milk mixture starts to gel, put in microwave and nuke for 10 seconds to liquefy again. When firm, cut into squares. Place squares on a pretty plate and serve.

What a coincidence to find out that Ann had also taken piano lessons from Jean Bossing as a child too. She also remembers her mother, Maxine Skaw, Jean Bossing and Sally Ripley teaching Sunday school classes in their homes before the Methodist Church was built in Lincoln.

Well, I have certainly gotten off the subject here. I started this section with tidbits about cooking with eggs and wandered from that to Jean, piano lessons, oatmeal cookies, lard, powdered milk, cats and dogs and finally to my friend Ann and her husband and our families. That is how my mind works now with advancing age. I just can't help but be amazed at how Jean's presence in our lives made such an impact so many years ago.

It is also quite amazing that Jeans passions for the Lord, family, friends, music and nursing also became my passions. It is those same passions that helped Ann and I to find each other as friends so many years later. We can't help but marvel how a person who influenced my life was also there for Ann and her family. How that all came around full circle, so that Ann and her family were there to instill a passion for the Lord, family, friends and music in my children's lives, is truly a miracle.

Ann Ward and I still keep in touch and compare notes about our grown children and grandchildren. My daughter Lana used to be great friends with the Ward children, but they have all grown and gone their separate ways. Lana now hangs out with a new set of friends, her husband, Jason, and sons Dawson and Bridger.

So with all that said, I will try to get back to cooking with eggs and using them for baking and making treats.

Another of my favorite cookbooks is *Betty Crocker's Picture Cook Book* It was my grandmother's cookbook, and it was her favorite. I am sure it is now an antique, as it was the first edition, published in 1950 by General Mills, Inc. I still use this cookbook frequently, but take better care of it now days. I plan to hand it down to a daughter or granddaughter one of these days. I have referenced *Betty Crocker's Picture Cook Book* on the following pages for tips on cooking and storing of eggs.

Jason and Lana Anderson Moyer and sons Dawson and Bridger (2011)

Mounds Bars

½ cup margarine softened
3 Tbsp. cocoa
1 cup chopped nuts
1 can (14 oz.) sweetened condensed milk
Dark chocolate, melted, optional
3 eggs
1¼ cups sugar
1 tsp. vanilla
1 cup flour
½ tsp. salt
2¼ cups coconut

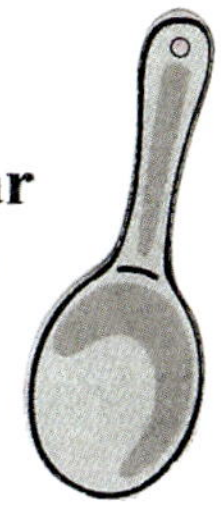

Heat oven to 350 degrees. In a bowl, mix together margarine, eggs, flour, salt, cocoa, sugar, nuts and vanilla. Pour and spread mixture evenly into a 9 x13-inch pan. Bake for 20 minutes. In another bowl, mix sweetened condensed milk with coconut. Spread evenly over cooked bar mixture in pan, and bake for an additional 15 minutes. Cool completely and then top with melted chocolate, if desired.

Homemade Sweetened Condensed Milk Donna Hammer Koss

Blend all ingredients in a blender:
⅓ cup boiling water
1 cup instant nonfat dry milk
2 Tbsp. melted butter
⅔ cup sugar

Oatmeal Pie

4 eggs beaten
1 cup quick oatmeal
1 cup chopped nuts
4 Tbsp. melted butter
⅔ cup brown sugar
2 to 3 Tbsp. evaporated milk
⅔ cup sugar
1 cup coconut

Mix all ingredients for 2-3 minutes. Pour into an unbaked prepared pie shell. Bake at 350 degrees for about 45 minutes. Serve with fresh or whipped cream.

Pie Crust Evelyn Hammer Young

4 cups flour
1 Tbsp. sugar
1½ tsp. salt
1½ cups shortening (Butter flavor Crisco) or lard for that 1950s secret ingredient

Blend all ingredients together with a pastry blender. Shortening should be no larger than pea size pieces. Place ¼ of mixture in a smaller mixing bowl and moisten with just enough cold water for easy mixing. Don't over mix, as dough will be tough. Roll out to the size of pie pan. Makes four crusts. **Note: For a richer dough for quiches or pot pies, use milk to moisten the dough**

Modern Day Recipe for a Perfect Pie Crust

4 cups flour
1 stick (½ cup) very cold butter
⅔ cup whole milk, very cold
1 Tbsp. sugar
½ cup very cold vegetable shortening
1 tsp. salt

Dice the butter and return it to the refrigerator while mixing the flour, salt and sugar in the bowl of a food processor, fitted with a steel blade and pulse a few times to mix. Add the butter and shortening. Pulse 8 to 12 times, until the butter is the size of peas. With the machine running, pour the ice water down the feed tube and pulse the machine until the dough begins to from a ball. Dump out on a floured board and roll into a ball. Wrap in plastic wrap and refrigerate for 30 minutes. Divide dough in half. Roll each piece on a well-floured board into a circle, rolling from the center to the edge, turning and flouring the dough to make sure it doesn't stick to the board. Fold the dough in half, place in a pie pan, and unfold to fit the pan. Repeat with top crust.

1. **Egg Yolks**—My mother says to throw them away because of the high cholesterol content. I say they must have a purpose (proper liver and nervous system function and hormone production). If I can't use them for puddings, baking or egg salad, then I feed them to the dogs. Two yolks can be used for one whole egg in custards and cream pie fillings. Two yolks and 1 teaspoon water can be used for one whole egg in cookies and dough.

2. **Egg Whites**—My mother's specialty is angel food cake. She also uses lots of egg whites for cakes and meringues. In order for egg whites to beat properly, they must be separated very carefully so as not to have any egg yolks in them and the bowl and beaters must be clean and dry. They must also warm to room temperature for thirty minutes before beating for highest volume. Egg whites will keep in the refrigerator for up to two weeks if covered tightly. My mother also says angel food cakes are very healthy since there is no fat in them and the egg whites are the purest form of protein. Her cake may be fat free and high in protein, but it isn't calorie free due to the sugar and flour content. If you have ever eaten my mom's angel food cake though, you soon forget about the calories. **It is the best.** *See page 36 for her recipe.*

3. There is a risk, though slight, that eggs and poultry can be contaminated with salmonella bacteria. The resulting food poisoning can be dangerous for infants, elderly and anyone that may be immunocompromised. I have many recipes from years back that call for raw egg whites, yolks or both. It is now advised to heat eggs for foods that will not be baked or cooked. Heating to above 160 degrees F. will kill the bacteria. Refrigeration to below 40 degrees F. will not allow the bacteria to grow, if it is present. If the bacteria is present, it is more likely concentrated in the yolk, so whites are safer to use. It is advised to cook them alone or separated, depending on their use. I have found that heating in the microwave is the best way to go, with at least fifteen seconds for an egg white or just until the edges are no longer translucent. Egg yolks can cook a little longer but just enough so that they are still runny. I haven't found any information as yet on using raw eggs in baking from my old cookbooks, so I had to turn to the internet for this latest information.

I have been looking for recipes that feature oatmeal and powdered milk for this section, along with egg recipes, as a remembrance of Jean Bossing. I have not been able to come up with anything that lard would be useful for other than the recipe on the next page and the pie crust recipe on a previous page.

Oils on canvas by Donna Hammer Koss

Eggshell Suet Cakes are for the Birds

1 cup lard
⅓ cup sugar
⅔ cup chicken feed
⅓ cup egg shells, washed, dried and crushed
1 cup chunky peanut butter
2 cups rolled oats
1 cup flour
2 cups yellow cornmeal

Melt lard over low heat. Add peanut butter. Stir until melted. Add other ingredients and mix well. Line a baking pan with wax paper. Spread into pan and then cut mixture into squares. Freeze for about an hour. Remove cakes and store in freezer. There is no need to thaw before serving. Just put them out and enjoy watching your feathered friends.

Homemade Bird Seed Wreath

¾ cup flour
4 Tbsp. light corn syrup
4 cups of mixed bird seed
½ cup of warm water
1 pkg. unflavored gelatin
non stick cooking spray
a mold of some kind such as a bundt pan—something with a hole in the center

In a large mixing bowl, add the warm water then sprinkle on the gelatin and mix well, then add the corn syrup and flour and stir until mixed. It will resemble a paste. Stir in the bird seed. Spray the mold or bundt cake pan with the non-stick spray so that the bird seed wreath doesn't stick and break. Start pressing in the mixture firmly. A layer at a time may work best to get it firmly pressed down into the mold Leave it overnight, and then the next day gently turn over the mold and the bird seed wreath should slip out onto a cooling rack. Leave it for a few more hours until the underside is totally hard. You will need something around it so that you can hang it on a tree. Try and find a place that you can see your feathered friends enjoying their treats!

Sun Beam Angel Food Cake Evelyn Hammer Young

1 cup + 2 Tbsp. cake flour
¾ cup powdered sugar
1½ cups egg whites (about 12) at room temperature
1½ tsp. cream of tartar
1 cup sifted granulated
½ tsp. salt
1 tsp. vanilla extract
1 tsp. almond extract

Sift cake flour and powdered sugar together 4 times and set bowl aside. In a mixing bowl, beat egg whites, cream of tartar and salt on medium speed until soft peaks form. Add granulated sugar, 2 tablespoons at a time, beating well after each addition; beat until glossy and stiff peaks form. Add extracts on low speed. Gently fold powdered sugar and cake flour into egg mixture.

Pour into an ungreased 10-inch tube pan, gently cutting through batter to help spread it in the pan. Bake on the lowest rack at 375 degrees for 30 to 35 minutes or until top crust is golden brown and cracks feel dry. Immediately turn cake upside down to cool for 30 minutes. If cake pan does not have "legs" on top, place cake over a pop bottle. Run knife around edge and center of cake and push out.

Angel Food Cake Frosting

1½ cups powdered sugar
hot water-enough to make a glaze
¼ cup butter
1 tsp. almond extract

Mix all together until smooth. Add: **½ cup chopped nuts**

Eggnog Chocolate Cake

11 to 12 egg yolks
2 cups sugar
3 squares melted chocolate
2 cups sour cream or buttermilk
1 tsp. vanilla extract
2½ cups flour
1 tsp. baking powder
2 tsp. baking soda
¼ tsp. nutmeg
1 tsp. rum extract

Beat egg yolks until light. Add sugar and mix well. Add the melted chocolate and mix. Add buttermilk or sour cream alternately with sifted dry ingredients. Mix well and add flavorings. Bake in an angel food cake pan with enough batter left for 1½ dozen cupcakes. Bake at 350 degrees for 40 minutes or until done for cake and 15 to 20 minutes for cupcakes.

Coconut Cream Pie

1 (13.5 oz.) can coconut milk
2 eggs + 1 egg yolk, beaten
½ cup corn starch
2 cups sweetened flaked coconut, divided
1 deep dish pie shell, baked and cooled
2 Tbsp. powdered sugar
1½ cups half-and-half
¾ cup granulated sugar
¼ tsp. salt
1 tsp. coconut or vanilla extract
1 cup heavy whipping cream
1 tsp. vanilla or coconut extract

Combine coconut milk, half and half, eggs, sugar, corn starch and salt in a large, microwave safe bowl (Pyrex). Stir. Microwave on high for one minute, stir. Repeat until a thick custard has developed, about 5 to 7 minutes. Stir in 1½ cups coconut and coconut extract. Pour custard into a cooled pie shell. Refrigerate for at least 2 hours.

Preheat oven to 350 degrees. Spread coconut on baking sheet and bake for 5 to 7 minutes stirring occasionally, until golden brown. Whip heavy cream until soft peaks form. Add in sugar and extract and continue whipping until stiff. Spread whipped cream on top of coconut custard and sprinkle with toasted coconut. Refrigerate.

Coconut Macaroons

Evelyn Hammer Young

½ cup chopped nuts
3 egg whites
1 (14 oz.) bag coconut
1 (14 oz.) can sweetened condensed milk
1 packet saltine crackers or 1 cup corn flakes (crushed)

Brown nuts and coconut in a 350 degree oven for 10 to15 minutes; stir frequently. Whip the egg whites and blend in the sweetened condensed milk. Add the browned coconut and nuts and crushed crackers to the egg mixture. Drop by teaspoonfuls on greased cookie sheet (parchment paper on the cookie sheet works good for these). Bake for 12 to 14 minutes at 350 degrees.

Impossible Custard Pie

4 eggs or 8 egg yolks
½ tsp. salt
1 tsp. vanilla extract
½ cup Bisquick
1 cup sugar
¼ tsp. nutmeg
2⅔ cup milk
1 cup coconut

Put all ingredients in a blender and mix well. Pour into a greased 9-inch pie pan. Sprinkle with nutmeg. Bake for 15 minutes at 450 degrees then 350 degrees to finish for 35 to 40 minutes or until knife inserted into side of filling comes out clean.

The painting below, titled Historic Lincoln by Robert Morgan depicts Lincoln as it looked about 1939. Bob Morgan was commissioned to paint the picture, using an old photograph as a guide, to help the community of Lincoln celebrate its Centennial Celebration in 1989. Many prints of Historic Lincoln were sold by members of the Lincoln Historical Society to help commemorate the celebration for that year. Bob Morgan became a personal friend to many in the Lincoln, Helena and Great Falls areas through his artwork and outgoing and generous personality. All the original buildings from that early period have been replaced or destroyed by fire over the years.

The top photo, on the next page, was a postcard found by Cathie Petek in her family's treasures, which must have been taken around 1949. It shows the original Stoner's Store, the newly replaced Lincoln Hotel, the Phillips 66 station and the Corner Bar, which burned down shortly thereafter.

The lower right photo shows Lambkin's Bar and Café built about 1952 by Donald Hammer. Lambkin's Bar and Café and Hotel are the only structures still standing from that early 1950s era.

Lincoln Stage parked in front of garage and Stoner's Store (1949)

Lincoln, Montana

Drawing by June Petek

Another favorite memory of June Petek was her ability to ice-skate. June, who was very active in the Lincoln community, was always smiling, laughing and loving to all who knew her. She had more talent than anyone I knew, and she was always willing to teach and show others how to do things in a ladylike style. With her elegance and grace, she was the Dorothy Hamill of the 1950s era.

During a visit with Butch Gehring some years back, I informed him about June's battle with cancer. The first thing he said was, "I remember her so well. She was the neat lady who taught us all to ice-skate." June was instrumental in getting our community leaders to build an ice-skating rink for us children to enjoy during the long winter months. She was able to get the fire department to flood the corner of Main Street (Highway 200) and Stemple Road where the Texaco station was later built. We would sweep the snow off after school, and some adult, usually June, would help us get a fire going where we could warm up, roast marshmallows and hot dogs and enjoy hot chocolate and cookies.

Proverbs 31: 25, 31 "She is a woman of strength and dignity, and has no fear of old age. When she speaks, her words are wise, and kindness is the rule for everything she says. Praise her for the many fine things she does. These good deeds of hers shall bring her honor and recognition from people of importance."

x This brings so many warm memories of all "my Lincoln kids," & our skating in good old Lincoln.

June showed all the children in our community love and respect. I just wish we could have shown her our appreciation for the impact she made on our lives before she passed on to be with the Lord in 2008. The note above was on the front of a cute Christmas card June sent in 2003 in her beautiful handwriting.

I was so hooked on ice-skating that I would skate to the post office to pick up the mail and skate back home again. I never got hurt on the ice rink, but did fall off the steps of the post office, which was then located in the Lincoln Mercantile. Even though I heard my arm break, I didn't want anyone to see me crying from the pain and embarrassment. So I just got up as best I could with one arm and skated back home. Since this was before we had Dr. Smith in our midst, my parents had to take me to Great Falls to have my arm set and a cast applied. My mother was quite frightened by the whole situation and had to call upon her friend June, who helped her put an ice pack on my arm and elevate it on pillows before taking me to the hospital.

Hot Chocolate Mix

1 (8 qt. size) powdered milk (9 cups dry)
1 (12 oz.) jar non-dairy creamer, powder
2½ cups powdered sugar
2 pound carton Nestlé's Quik

Mix all ingredients together in a very large bowl. Transfer to a storage container or ice cream bucket when mixed. Mark with the directions for mixing, which are: Add about ⅓ cup of mix to a cup of hot water and stir well.

Rich Hot Cocoa

¾ cup cocoa
1 tsp. powdered vanilla
2 pounds powdered sugar
1 cup powdered cream
6 cups powdered milk
½ bag (8 oz.) miniature marshmallows
¼ tsp. salt

Mix all ingredients as above. Add ⅓ cup of mix to a cup of hot water and stir.

Spiced Apple Cider

2 quarts apple cider or juice
4 cinnamon sticks
16 whole cloves
½ cup brown sugar
1 tsp. whole allspice

Simmer in a crock-pot until ready to serve or at least for 15 minutes. Strain. If desired, add **1 medium orange**, sliced thin.

Make-Ahead Eggnog

6 cups whole milk
1 tsp. pumpkin pie spice
1 cup egg substitute
2 tsp. rum extract
⅔ cup sugar
French Vanilla whipped topping, optional

In a 3-quart slow cooker, combine first five ingredients. Cover and cook on low for 2 to 3 hours or until heated through. Serve eggnog in mugs; dollop with whipped topping and sprinkle with additional pumpkin pie spice if desired.

Speaking of Dorothy Hamill, our Olympic figure skating champion from the 1970s era, check out this photo of Cathie Petek Beard and see if she and Dorothy don't share a striking resemblance both in appearance and as "go-getters" in a world of women making things happen.

Cathie and Bud Beard

Peppermint Hot Chocolate

½ cup crushed peppermint candies or canes
1 box instant chocolate pudding mix
11 oz. powdered coffee creamer
11 cups dry milk powder
1½ cups powdered sugar
4 Tbsp. cocoa
2 pounds hot chocolate mix (Nestlé's Quik)

Crush candy in a bag or food processor to a fine powder.
Mix all ingredients together in a large bowl.
To make a cup of hot chocolate, use ⅓ cup powder mix to ⅔ cup hot water. Store in an airtight container.

Red Hot Cinnamon Apple Cider

Simmer **2 quarts apple cider** in a crock-pot. When hot, add about **¼ cup red-hot cinnamon candies**, more or less to taste. When candies are melted, it is ready to serve.

When we went to Augusta to attend high school, we were known as "the Lincoln Stump Jumpers" since we came from a logging community. We found a pond at the bottom of the dump and cemetery hill and cleaned off the snow for our ice-skating rink. Since we couldn't get rid of some of the tree branches sticking out of the ice, we would try to jump over them. We gave them good reason to call us that name. Augusta kids wanted to join in our fun but weren't too thrilled with skating. They soon started dragging old tires over from the dump and used them, along with some gasoline, to try to impress us with their fire-starting techniques. They made such a mess that we had to abandon that skating pond.

Percy (the cat) and Karleen with skating injury

Joyce Bean (Shaw) felt bad for us and soon began hosting ice-skating parties at Bean Lake. She enjoyed ice-skating as much as we did and helped us to fit into the Augusta scene. Leaving home at age fourteen, to stay in Augusta all week, was a rather lonely and frightening experience. We were all blessed with caring families who took us in and provided for us.

Joyce and her parents went to a lot of trouble and expense to feed and entertain all of us. We got to have our fire with hot dogs, hot chocolate and marshmallows, just like in Lincoln. Joyce has remained a close friend to many of us, and we still continue to get together to this day.

Proverbs 31:19 "She provides for the poor, and generously helps those in need. She has no fear of winter for her household, for she has made warm clothes for all of them."

Diana Welch Fleming (Colton) has been a close friend with Joyce since high school. Their husbands were friends in the Air Force at Malmstrom Air Force Base in Great Falls, Montana, when the girls met them. (I will share more about Diana in a later section with a story about Evelyn and Gary Holm, her parents from Lincoln.) I later married one of the non-skating, cowboy types from Augusta, known for his tire-dragging and fire-starting skills.

Joyce Bean Shaw, Diana Welch Colton and Karleen Hammer Anderson

Pigs in Bacon *Better Homes and Gardens Jr. Cookbook*

8 to 12 frankfurters (hotdogs) - slit each one to make a pocket. Don't cut through.

2 to 3 slices of processed cheese - cut each slice into 4 even pieces. Place a piece of cheese into slit in each hotdog.

8 to 12 slices of bacon - wrap a slice around each hotdog like a spiral. Fasten with a toothpick at each end. Bake at 350 degrees for 17 minutes. Turn at "half time." Remove the toothpicks and serve on a hotdog bun or roll (8 to 12) with mustard or chili sauce.

Franks and Beans

1 large can baked beans or pork and beans

1 pound of frankfurters (hotdogs) – sliced lengthwise into thirds

2 Tbsp. catsup **1 tsp. dry mustard**

1 Tbsp. brown sugar **2 to 3 strips of bacon**

Place ⅓ of baked beans in a 1½ quart casserole dish. Place a layer of sliced hotdogs, half of them, over the beans. Cover with more beans but save some for the top. Add the catsup and mustard to that layer of beans and then add the rest of the hotdog slices. Add the rest of the beans over the hotdogs and top with the brown sugar. Place bacon slices on top. Bake covered for 30 minutes at 350 degrees.

German Pizza Betty McBratney/Augusta & Conrad, Mt.
My Augusta mother during high school

6 large potatoes, peeled and thinly sliced **Salt and pepper to taste**

1 large onion, chopped **6 eggs, beaten**

Oil for frying **Bell pepper slices, green, red or yellow**

6 hotdogs or 1 large Kielbasa sausage or canned Spam, cut into slices

2 cups grated cheese, Cheddar, Swiss, Mozzarella or sliced Velveeta

In a large skillet, cook potatoes and onions in enough oil to prevent sticking. Cover with a lid and cook over low heat until almost done. Stir frequently to cook evenly. Season with salt and pepper. When potatoes are almost cooked, flatten with spatula and cover with sliced hotdogs or sausage or Spam. Pour beaten eggs over the meat and cook until eggs begin to get firm. Cover with a cheese and continue to cook until cheese is melted. Place pepper slices on top of the cheese. Cut into wedges like a pizza and serve from the frying pan.

Little Smokies (Grandson Seth's favorite recipe since hotdogs and pork are his favorite foods)

1 package precooked Little Smokies sausages

1 bottle Barbeque sauce

Place Little Smokies in a small crock-pot. Pour barbeque sauce over the sausages. Cover and heat. When ready to serve, pickup with round toothpick.

Corn Dogs in a Cup

1 cup ground cornmeal **¾ cup butter, melted**

2 cups white flour **1½ cups sugar**

1 Tbsp. baking powder **4 egg, separated**

½ tsp. salt **1 cup milk**

1 tsp. vanilla **1 Tbsp. molasses**

Combine cornmeal, flour, baking powder, salt and sugar. Combine egg yolks, milk, vanilla, molasses and butter. Stir into dry ingredients until thoroughly moistened. Beat egg whites until stiff and *carefully* fold into the batter. Fill cupcake tins ½ full of batter. Place 2-3 one inch slices of **hotdogs** over the batter. Top with batter to almost fill the cupcake tin. Bake at 350 degrees for 25 minutes.

We don't do the ice skating thing anymore but still hike and picnic in the mountains behind the Bean Ranch. We also have BBQs (where we include our husbands), shopping trips and ladies retreats. We get together more now since our children are raised and gone.

When Joyce and her husband Virgil retired, they moved back to the Bean home place. They then remodeled and added on to the original house. They also cared for Fern, Joyce's mother, until she died in 2005. Joyce volunteered one day a week to cook for students and staff at the C-N Wilderness BibleCollege, which is just up the road from her home. Joyce also packed in food and supplies, on horseback, for students when they were on hikes and wilderness journeys.

The students loved Joyce's homemade cookies. Her mothers recipe for raisin oatmeal cookies and chocolate chip cookies were a big hit. What a coincidence to come across almost the same recipe by Alice Evans in *The Lincoln Cookbook.*

Joyce Bean Shaw

Fern's Boiled Raisin Oatmeal Cookies — Fern Bean/Joyce Bean Shaw

1 cup Crisco or ½ margarine and ½ Crisco
2 cups sugar
3 egg, beaten
2½ cups raisins, boiled
1 cup raisin juice
3 cups oatmeal
3 cups flour
2 tsp. baking soda
1 tsp. nutmeg
1 tsp. cloves
½ tsp. salt
1 cup salted peanuts or walnuts

Boil raisins in water; cool. Sift dry ingredients. Cream shortening and sugar. Add eggs and cooled raisin juice alternately with dry ingredients. Add oats, raisins and nuts last. Bake at 375 for 10 minutes. Makes about 6 dozen cookies. (If you find they spread to much after the first pan bakes, then add a little more flour to the remaining mixture).

Jumbo Raisin Cookies — Alice Evans, *Old Lincoln Cookbook*

Boil for 5 minutes: **2 cups raisin or dates and 1 cup cold water**

Cream: **1 cup shortening**, **2 cups sugar**, **3 beaten eggs**, **1 tsp. vanilla**

Sift together: **4 cups flour**, **1 tsp. baking powder**, **1½ tsp. cinnamon**, **1 tsp. baking soda**, **¼ tsp. nutmeg**, **1 tsp. salt**, **¼ tsp. allspice**

Add dry ingredients alternately to creamed mixture with raisin water. When mixed well, add **raisins and 1 cup chopped nuts.** Chill. Drop on cookie sheet by teaspoons. Bake 350-400 degrees 12 to 15 minutes.

Chocolate Chip Oatmeal Cookies

Cream:
1 cup margarine
1¼ cup brown sugar
½ cup sugar
2 Tbsp. milk
2 tsp. vanilla
2 eggs

Sift together:
1¾ cup flour
1 tsp. baking soda
½ teaspoon salt

Add at end:
1 (12 oz.) pkg. chocolate chips
2½ cups oatmeal
1 cup nuts (opt.)

Add flour mixture to creamed ingredients
Add and mix in other dry ingredients. Bake at 375 degrees for 10 min.

Happy Trails Snack Mix — Joyce Bean Shaw

3 cups miniature pretzels
1 to 2 packages milk chocolate M&M's
2 cups mixed nuts
1 cup chopped dried apples (opt.)
1 cup peanuts
1 cup Chex cereal
1 cup raisins

Combine all ingredients in a large bowl. Store in an airtight container. Put in sandwich bags for hikes and trail rides.

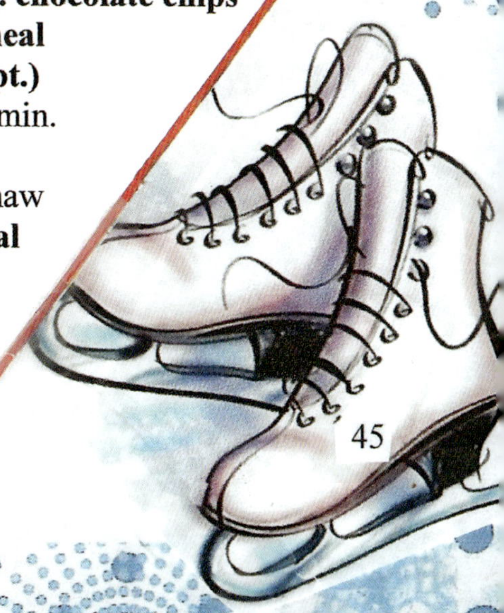

Although I didn't know Alice Evans well, her daughter Pat and I became close friends while in high school at Augusta. We were roommates the four years we were away at Augusta. Joyce and Pat became good friends then also. They roomed together at collage while attending MSU in Bozeman and later worked together in Great Falls. Just as Joyce returned to Augusta after retiring, Pat returned to Lincoln after she retired to help care for her mother until her death in 2008. Pat lived near her mother in Lincoln in the summers and then they would both travel to Arizona for the winter.

I don't remember Pat's mother hosting any parties for us kids, but there were parties at the Evans house when the parents, Don and Alice, were gone. These parties, hosted by Pat and her brother Mike, could get a little rowdy. It didn't take Pat's parents long to realize they maybe shouldn't travel and leave the kids home alone.

Joyce Bean

I do remember one outing at the Evans place at Patterson Prairie where Don Evans ran a sawmill. Mike was driving with two sleds behind his car. One sled was on a short rope with two of us kids on it. The other sled was a toboggan on a long rope with several kids on it. Of course, I fell off the sled and got run over by the toboggan. My injuries were minor. It was just another time that I knew God was watching over us.

The Evans family, like so many other Lincoln families, also endured heartache. Pat's brother, Mike, died in a tragic car accident when he was just a teenager. He is still remembered by many of us who visit his grave at the Old Lincoln Cemetery.

Pat Evans

Graduation photos taken from the Augusta High School annual the "Wapiti" 1965

It has been fun to visit with Pat on some of our Lincoln visits and class reunions. We had quite an adventure finding her home outside of Lincoln. My husband thought we were on another wild goose chase when we first tried to find it. What a treat to find her beautiful log home way out in the country.

Pat bakes great chocolate chip cookies and has fun visiting about the old days in her cozy log home around the woodstove. Pat knew the legendary Fanny Steele, who was the first lady bronc riding champion. Fanny was from the Lincoln/Ovando area and a neighbor of the Evans family. Pat still uses some of Fanny Steele's original old-time recipes.

Although Pat wasn't part of June Petek's original group of ice-skating students, it didn't take her long to learn. She was also a quick learner in school as well. She was valedictorian of our 1965 Augusta High School senior class of eighteen graduates, five of whom were students from Lincoln. There were about twenty Lincoln students attending Augusta High School during those few years that we were there.

Sour Cream Raisin Bars

2 cups raisins
1¾ cup rolled oats
1¾ cup flour
1 tsp. baking soda
1 cup brown sugar
1 tsp. cinnamon
1 cup butter, softened
3 egg yolks
1½ cups sour cream
1 cup sugar
2½ Tbsp. cornstarch
1 tsp. vanilla

Heat oven to 350 degrees. Line a 9 x 13-inch baking pan with parchment paper and spray with cooking spray. Cover the raisins with hot water and let soak until plump about 5 to10 minutes. Drain and set aside.

Crumble together the oats, flour, soda, brown sugar, cinnamon and butter in a large bowl. Pat half of the mixture on prepared pan. Bake at 350 degrees for 5 minutes. Remove from oven and set aside. Meanwhile, whisk egg yolks, sour cream, sugar and cornstarch in a medium saucepan over medium heat. Stir constantly until mixture thickens, about 10 minutes. Remove from heat and stir in vanilla and raisins. Pour the filling over partially baked crust. Sprinkle remaining oat mixture over the filling. Lightly pat down. Bake at 325 degrees for about 30 minutes until top is browned. Let cool. Remove from pan using parchment paper handles. Cut into bars and serve. Refrigerate if not eating right away. Top with whipped cream.

Rhubarb Oatmeal Bars

1½ cups unsifted flour
½ tsp. salt
½ tsp. cinnamon
1½ cups oatmeal (old fashioned)
1 cup packed brown sugar
¾ cup soft butter

Mix above ingredients and then add the butter to form coarse crumbs. Press half of the crumb mixture into the bottom of a greased 9 x 13-inch pan. Spread rhubarb sauce onto crumb layer.

Rhubarb Sauce:

1 pound chopped rhubarb **½ cup sugar** **⅛ tsp. cinnamon**

Heat above ingredients to boiling. Cover and simmer 5 to 8 minutes. Thicken mixture with: **1 tablespoon cornstarch in 2 tablespoons water** and stir into hot rhubarb mix. Cool. Top sauce with remaining crumbs and **¼ cup walnuts**. Bake for 25 to 30 minutes at 375 degrees. Cool before cutting into bars.

Peppermint Wafer Dessert

½ pound peppermint stick candy
½ cup light cream
½ Tbsp. (½ envelope) unflavored gelatin
in 2 Tbsp. cold water
1 (9 or 10 oz.) pkg. chocolate wafers, crushed
1½ cups heavy cream, whipped

Crush candy, add light cream and heat in double boiler until candy dissolves. Add gelatin softened in cold water, chill until partially set. Fold in the whipped cream. Spread part of the crushed chocolate wafers in a 9 x 9-inch buttered pan; then pour over the candy-cream mixture, and put remaining wafers on top; or form alternate layers.

"Haystack Butte" by Gus Wolfe

I am always reminded of Joyce and Pat whenever I see Haystack Butte, another popular mountain that can be seen clearly from anywhere in the Augusta area as another part of the Rocky Mountain Front. Climbing Haystack Butte was the ultimate goal of all Augusta kids. It must have been a rite of passage to accomplish this feat, and the Lincoln kids accepted the challenge. It seems to me that Joyce was the instigator of what was supposed to be a quick after-school activity one weekday in 1962.

With no preparation or planning, about sixteen adventurous Augusta and Lincoln youths headed out in the back of two pickups driven by Joyce Bean and Rick Mirehouse. A group of boys went around the north side to climb, and the rest of us, mostly girls, went up the south side which is all shale and very difficult to climb. We did make it to the top before sunset, with the north face climbers already there waiting for us. Of course they had packed the only water and a few candy bars, which were gone by the time we arrived.

It was a beautiful site on top of the peak, but we couldn't stay long due to nightfall approaching. If we thought climbing up was hard, it was a piece of cake compared to sliding down in the dark. By the time we arrived in Augusta, it was well past midnight. The parents were up in arms and had sent out the law (Jack Walsh) to find us. We were all cold and hungry but thrilled that we had safely accomplished such a great adventure.

Pat Evans didn't fare so well. By the time we got off that mountain, about all that was left of her tennis shoes were the shoelaces.

HAYRIDE HELD AT BEAN'S

Twenty students attended a hayride, hosted by Joyce Bean, Wednesday, February 5. The guests met at the Bean Ranch at 6:00 p.m. where they piled into a truck bed filled with hay and traveled several miles past Bean's.

After building a bonfire, Mrs. Jean Barrett and Mrs. Fern Bean arrived with hot dogs, potato chips, and cocoa.

After lunch the students again piled in the truck to return to their homes.

This is an article from the Augusta High Schools weekly newspaper, the "Lariat", from about 1963.

Munchy Crunchy Cookies

1 cup butter
1 cup sugar
1 cup brown sugar
2 eggs
2 cups flour
1 tsp. baking powder
½ tsp. baking soda
½ tsp. salt
1 tsp. vanilla
2 cups quick oats
4 Tbsp. coconut
1½ cups chocolate chips

Sift dry ingredients together. Cream sugars, butter, eggs and vanilla. Add sifted ingredients. Add chips, oatmeal and coconut. Place by teaspoonfuls on greased cookie sheets. Bake 10 to 12 minutes at 350 degrees.

Sugar Raisin Drops

Better Homes and Gardens Jr. Cookbook

1⅓ cup shortening
3 Tbsp. milk
2 tsp. baking powder
1½ cups sugar
3 cups flour
1 cup raisins
2 eggs
½ tsp. salt
1 cup chopped nuts

Cream shortening and sugar. Add eggs. Beat until fluffy. Add vanilla and milk to shortening mixture. Sift dry ingredients and add to mixture, then add nuts and raisins. Drop on greased cookie sheet by teaspoons. Bake 12 minutes at 375 degrees. Remove cookies from pan and sprinkle with sugar.

Baked Oatmeal

Terri Erickson & Joyce Bean/C-N Bible College

2 cups oatmeal
1 tsp. cinnamon
½ cup butter, melted
1 cup brown sugar
1 tsp. salt
2 eggs, beaten
2 tsp. baking powder
1 cup milk

Combine all ingredients. Spoon into greased 9 x 9-inch square pan. Bake at 350 degrees for 40 to 45 minutes. Top with whipped cream and fresh fruit. Good for breakfast or brunch.

Oatmeal Muffins

1 cup sifted flour
½ tsp. baking soda
2 tsp. baking powder
½ tsp. cinnamon
½ tsp. salt
1 cup quick oats
½ cup brown sugar
1 cup buttermilk
¼ cup cooking oil
1 egg beaten

Sift dry ingredients together. Combine oats, brown sugar and buttermilk in bowl. Let stand 10 minutes. Add egg and oil; mix well. Add dry ingredients, stirring just enough to moisten. Spoon batter into greased 2½-inch muffin pan cups, filling ⅔ full. Bake at 375 degrees for 25 minutes.

Many pictures of the Bean Ranch and Joyce feature Steamboat Mountain in the background. This 8,579-foot mountain is part of the Rocky Mountain Front and a beginning to the Scapegoat Wilderness area. This area may become part of the Scapegoat/Bob Marshall Wilderness area in the near future.

The Steamboat Mountain area is a popular hiking, hunting, fishing and horseback riding area. Joyce has a great love of horses, and riding in the mountains is one of her passions. Visiting with Joyce as a teenager usually involved some sort of an adventure involving horses, whether herding cattle for her dad, Wallace, or trail rides on the trail toward Steamboat Mountain.

Joyce and Virgil took in two foreign exchange students several years back who attended Augusta High School. Daniel, who was from Mexico, stayed on with Virgil and Joyce and attended the C-N Wilderness Bible College. The school was established by Phyllis and Warren Barrett in memory of their son Steven. It is now a main bible college of the northwestern United States and attracts students from all over the country to study there.

Daniel and Joyce

Daniel met and later married Joyce's niece, Corrie, at the Bean Ranch in a ceremony in Joyce's yard. At Corrie and Daniel's wedding, a most unusual event occurred. Corrie washed the feet of her new husband, Daniel. Now most people at the wedding didn't understand the symbolism this act of love portrayed, but I saw it clearly. It portrayed the humility and submissive nature of Christ as he shows his love for others by being a servant to them instead of the master. It reminds me of a book I like to read by Karen Mains titled; *Open Heart, Open Home: The Hospitable Way to Make Others Feel Welcome and Wanted.* The author shares many stories, examples and Bible verses of how Christ taught his disciples to serve and care for others. She told about Jesus washing the feet of his disciples the last evening of his life and quotes John 13: 16 where Jesus stated, "*Truly, truly, I say to you, a servant is not greater than his master nor is he who is sent greater than he who sent him.*" (Mains, 1997, p. 69).

The author also states how servants create a home that people enjoy visiting, are reluctant to leave and enjoy a feeling of warmth toward each other with lots of laughter and sometimes singing and prayer. She also states: "If the food has been prepared or creatively served, so much the better." (Mains, 1997, p. 79).

I have observed so many Lincoln and Augusta women who made it their life's purpose to serve others. And this was the simple principle that Corrie and Daniel Meza displayed at their wedding on a warm July day in 2011, in Joyce's yard, with Steamboat Mountain in the background.

Daniel now attends a bible college in Bozeman, Montana that my friends Ann and Ron Ward helped establish when they were living in Bozeman. Remember Ann and I had the same piano teacher in Lincoln as children.

S'mores Crumb Bars

Jackie Barrett
Augusta, Montana

3 cups graham cracker crumbs
⅓ cup sugar ¾ cup butter, melted
3 cups miniature marshmallows
2 cups (12 oz.) semisweet or milk chocolate chips

Combine the crumbs, butter and sugar; press half into a greased 9 x 13-inch baking pan. Sprinkle with chips and marshmallows. Top with remaining crumb mixture; press firmly. Bake at 375 degrees for 10 minutes. Remove from the oven and immediately press top firmly with spatula. Cool completely. Cut into bars.

Caramel Apple Bars

Crust:

½ cup butter **¼ cup shortening** **1¾ cup flour**
1 cup brown sugar **1 cup oats** **1 tsp. salt**
½ tsp. baking soda **½ cup chopped pecans**

Filling:

4½ cup coarsely chopped peeled apples
3 Tbsp. flour
1 package caramels, melted or 1 jar caramel ice cream syrup

In a mixing bowl, cream butter, shortening and brown sugar until fluffy. Add flour, oats, salt and soda; mix well. Stir in pecans if desired. Set aside 2 cups. Press remaining oat mixture into the bottom of an ungreased 9 x 13-inch baking pan. For filling, toss apples with flour; spoon over the crust. Drizzle caramel over apples. Top with the reserved oat mixture. Bake at 400 degrees for 30 minutes.

Fudge Squares

Vernie Burns (see note below)
Old Lincoln Cookbook

½ cup butter **1½ cups sugar** **3 eggs**
3 squares chocolate (melted) **1 tsp. vanilla** **¾ cup flour**
½ tsp. salt **½ cup milk** **¾ cup chopped nuts (opt.)**

Cream butter and sugar. Add melted chocolate. Beat in eggs, one at a time, and vanilla. Sift salt with flour and add alternately with the milk. Add nuts. Spread into a greased 9 x 13-inch cake pan. Bake at 350 degrees for 35 minutes. Frost with recipe below.

Jackie and Dave Barrett

Frosting:

¼ cup milk **1 cup sugar**
¼ cup butter **1 square chocolate**

Boil 1 minute after mixture reaches boiling point; cool; beat until thick. Spread on cooled squares.

NOTE: Reece Burns, Vernie Burns' oldest son, was best friends with Mike Evans until his death. Reece has remained friends with Pat Evans and Joyce Bean since Augusta High School days.

Dave and Jackie Barrett at Corrie and Daniel's wedding

Joyce's love for horses, adventure, mountains and outdoor activities such as ice-skating and hayrides helped us to become part of the Augusta scene and enjoy our school days during those years.

Roadway near the Bean Ranch on a winter day in Augusta, Montana

I have one more adventure about Joyce that the picture above reminds me of. This photo, and the one of Haystack Butte on an earlier page, was taken by a classmate of ours and a friend to all in Augusta, Gus Wolfe. Gus is a neighbor to Joyce Bean and enjoys using his gift of photography by taking some beautiful photos around the Augusta area. This photo is of a roadway near the Bean Ranch on a cold windblown day. It seems the wind blows a lot in Augusta, and driving through snow drifts can be quite an art—one that Joyce has learned over the years, the hard way.

That adventure with Joyce began one wintery Saturday when Joyce invited Pat Evans and I and another girl from Augusta to come out to her home for the rest of the weekend for a slumber party and outdoor activities. Joyce was driving us back to her home and traveling along at a good clip when she hit one of those snow drifts. The car spun out of control, jumped over the drift and off the roadway then careened through the barrow pit and into the Barrett's hay field. The dilemma then became which one of us should walk to the Barrett's ranch house for help. Pat and I agreed to go because we were each wearing snow boots, warm pants, warm coats, caps, wool scarfs and warm mittens.

Dressing warm in winter weather was a strict rule at our home, and also with Pat and Joyce as well. My sister and I had some strange looking garbs during winter months when we would have to wear warm winter pants, even if wearing a dress, and either a sweater or sweat shirt under our coats for extra warmth giving us that "layered look." Mothers rules for warmth overshadowed any possibility of looking good or being in style. Donna and I also had to dress like that in the winter, in case of a situation just as the one we now found ourselves in. No cell phones back then either.

So Pat and I started out on our trek to the Barrett's, by following the roadway in the wind and snowdrifts. We were doing just fine, until we heard the other girls calling for us to turn around and go through the hayfield with them, as it would be a shortcut. I guess our Augusta friend, who wasn't

Honey Raisin Bars

Jackie Barrett
Augusta, Mt.

Sift:
3½ cups flour
2 tsp. baking soda
2 tsp. salt
3 tsp. cinnamon
1 tsp. cardamom, ground
1 tsp. nutmeg

Cream:
1½ cups shortening
1 cup sugar
1 cup brown sugar
3 eggs
1 cup honey

Add:
2 tsp. vanilla
2 cups raisins
1 cup nuts, chopped
1½ cup quick oats

Cream usual ingredients. Blend in sifted dry ingredients. Stir in vanilla, raisins, nuts and oats. Spread in two 10½ x 15-inch jelly roll pan. Bake at 375 degrees for 18 to 20 minutes. Sprinkle with **powdered sugar** when a bit cool.

Starlight Surprise Cookies

Jean Barrett
Augusta, Mt.

2 eggs
1 cup white sugar
½ cup brown sugar
1 cup shortening
3 cups flour
1 tsp. baking soda
½ tsp. salt
2 Tbsp. water
1 tsp. vanilla extract

Beat the eggs to creamy texture; slowly add in sugars; then shortening and beat for a minute; add flour mixture, mixing in the 2 tablespoons water, lastly add the vanilla. Make three rolls and put in wax paper. Chill overnight. Slice rolls and place a mint wafer between two slices. Seal edges and bake at 375 degrees for 10 to 12 minutes until lightly browned.

Blarney Stones

Jean Barrett

4 eggs
1 cup sugar
1 cup flour
1½ tsp. baking powder
¼ tsp. salt
½ cup boiling water
1 tsp. vanilla extract

Separate eggs; beat yolks until light and fluffy. Add sugar gradually; beat until creamy. Sift flour once and measure dry ingredients, add to flour and sift again. Add to egg mixture, alternately with boiling water. Blend in vanilla. Fold in egg whites (beaten). Put into a 7 x 14-inch baking pan and bake at 375 degrees about 25 minutes. When cool, cut into bars and frost with: **1 cup powdered sugar, ¼ cup butter and 1 tsp. vanilla extract.** Immediately roll in **ground salted peanuts.**

Photograph of Steamboat Mountain from Facebook profile of Jackie Barrett dressed for the weather and had no boots, decided we would take to long and she could make better time than we could by cutting across the field. By the time we reached the Barrett's house, our friend had the beginning of frostbite. Jean Barrett put warm water in the bathtub so our friend could put her feet and hands in to warm up. Jean sent the men, Bill, Joe, and Dave to get Joyce's car out of the snowdrift so we could recoup and be on our way again. Since we had already missed whatever we were in such a hurry to get to, we hung around for a while for hot chocolate and a few treats, which was Jean Barrett's style. She was a truly amazing and gracious lady.

Looking back at our grade school days in Lincoln, walking to and from school was our main mode of transportation. We didn't have school buses in Lincoln back then. Whenever Donna and I were running late for school, we had to do some jogging to make up the time. Hitching a ride with George Anderson, who drove his family in from the west end of the valley, got us there before the school bell rang on several occasions. It was about one mile from First Avenue to the school. Of course, our kids make fun of us now and say it was about five miles, snowing and uphill both ways.

Walking in Lincoln was an everyday occurrence. In addition to school, my mother, sister, dog and I would walk to the post office to get the mail every evening. Walking has always been and still is the best form of exercise for kids and adults alike. We have always known that walking not only helped make for strong hearts and lungs, but also helps to preserve bone and muscle mass.

There were other forms of exercise when we were growing up in Lincoln. Along with walking, skating, sledding, and baseball, there were the adventurous games we played in the woods around the school and our homes. There was Annie-I-Over, which consisted of launching a ball over some unsuspecting summer home owner's roof to friends on the other side. If the ball was caught, then it became a game of tag and they would run or try to sneak to the other side of the house to tag the throwing team. Donna and I especially liked to play that one over our house when our parents weren't home. It seemed they were a little too protective of their glass windows when they were at home.

The picture below shows the contrast of winter in Augusta, with the soft and quiet snowfall we had become accustomed to in Lincoln. Walking through those pine trees in Lincoln was such a peaceful experience, as it gave a person time to think, pray, reflect, and appreciate the beauty of God's creation. I especially love this closing picture, taken by my mother, looking down First Avenue toward Highway 200 on the roadway to our home. (Note our dog, Yogi, up the road))

Road to the Hammer home on a winter day in Lincoln, Montana

Popcorn Cake

6 to 8 cups popped corn
½ cup real butter
1 large bag marshmallows
1 to 2 cups small gumdrops
1 cup almonds or mixed nuts

Melt butter in 3 quart saucepan over low heat. Add marshmallows; stir occasionally until smooth. Remove from heat and stir in popcorn until well coated. Add cut-up small gum drops and nuts if desired. Press into a well-greased angel food cake pan. Push the coated corn into pan until well compacted. Refrigerate. When ready to serve, cut around the sides of pan and removed middle cone and invert onto a pretty cake plate.

Nellie's Caramels — Nellie Knight

1 pound brown sugar (2¼ cups)
1 cup butter
1 cup light corn syrup
1 (15 oz.) can sweetened condensed milk
1 tsp. vanilla extract

Melt butter in heavy 3 quart saucepan. Add sugar and vanilla. Stir thoroughly. Stir in corn syrup and mix well. Gradually add milk, stirring constantly. Cook and stir over med heat to firm ball stage (245 degrees). Nellie doesn't cook them to 245 degrees as she likes them softer.

Caramel Corn (My girls favorite and they called it "Sticky Pop Corn") Joyce Bean Shaw

8 to 10 cups popped corn
2 cups sugar
1 cup margarine
½ cup light corn syrup
1 tsp. vanilla extract
Almonds (opt.)

Cook sugar, butter (or margarine) and corn syrup, while popping the corn, to a soft ball stage. It doesn't take very long; I find it is done about the same time I am done popping the corn. Stir in the vanilla. Pour the syrup over the popcorn and nuts. I put popcorn into 2 very large bowls so there is room for stirring.

Ice Cream Floats — *Better Homes and Gardens Junior Cookbook*

Frosty Orange Float: Mix spoonful of orange sherbet and chilled orange in glass. Fill with pop. Float sherbet on top

Root beer Float: Mix vanilla ice cream with root beer as above. Fill with pop. Float ice cream on top.

Can also use coke, grape soda, or wild cherry Pepsi instead of root beer.

7-Up Float: Use any flavor ice cream, such as chocolate, strawberry or sherbet mixed with 7-Up as above.

Party Mix — Evelyn Hammer Young

¼ cup margarine
1 teaspoon Worcestershire sauce
½ teaspoon garlic salt
2 cups mixed nuts
2 cups bite size crispy wheat squares
2 cups bite size crispy rice squares
2 cups pretzel sticks
2 cups toasted oat cereal

Melt margarine or butter and combine with Worcestershire sauce, and garlic salt. Pour over combined remaining ingredients, mix lightly. Spread on ungreased 11x16-inch jelly roll pan. Bake at 250 degrees 1 hour, stirring occasionally.

There was a tragic turn of events for us Lincoln kids with our love for the sport of ice skating. We lost our skating rink so it could become the new Texaco station. Such a bummer. We were never sure who the culprit was who decided to turn our pond into a gas station. I never knew if it was John Petek or Bob McClure who was the instigator of that heartbreaking event. Come to find out I was wrong on both counts. It was George Stoner who owned a lot of property on the south side of Highway 200 and who was the owner of the land our skating rink was on. George Stoner was the founder and owner of Stoner's Store. June and John Petek were buying the store from George. June helped run the store and John ran the gas pumps and stage line. John then built the new Texaco with George Stoner being the money man behind the adventure. Prior to building the Texaco station, John built a garage between Stoner's Store and the new site of the Texaco (our ice rink).

I read a book several years ago about Ted Kaczynski (aka "The Unabomber") which was written by his neighbor Chris Waits.

John Petek and friend loading a delivery truck in front of Stoner's Store

Old-time garage built and operated by John Petek

John Petek in front of the Texaco station

Chris described some of his adventures of living near Ted. He also told about using John's old garage as an arts center where he taught music lessons. Chris is married to Betty Jean Orr, a longtime friend of my sister and I while growing up in Lincoln. I don't know if Chris still owns the building, but it remains as a legacy to John Petek and is one of the only buildings still left in its original condition from those early days in Lincoln. I bet if John were here today he would have reopened it and named it "Petek's Pancake and Pastry Pub" knowing of his love for sweets and treats.

Stoner's Store and Stage Stop

Photo from "Story of Lincoln"–A Montana Centennial Project by the Pinegrove Extension Homemakers, 1989

Frosted Cinnamon Rolls

¼ cup butter, melted
¼ cup warm water
½ pkg. vanilla pudding
1 cup milk
1 egg, beaten
1 Tbsp. sugar
½ tsp. salt
4 cups bread flour
2½ tsp. yeast

Put ingredients in bread machine in order listed. Set machine on dough cycle. When dough comes out roll out into a large rectangle. Put the filling on top.

Filling:

½ cup butter, softened
2 Tbsp. cinnamon
1 cup brown sugar

Roll up the dough starting at the shorter end. Pinch to seal. Using dental floss cut rolls and place in greased jelly roll pan. Let dough rise until double in size. Bake at 350 degrees for 25 to 30 minutes.

Frosting: 4 oz. cream cheese **½ cup butter** **1½ cups powdered sugar**
½ tsp. vanilla extract **1½ tsp. milk** Mix and spread over warm rolls.

Whoop! I goofed!! I cut off John Petek's head with my Kodak Instamatic camera and my 1960s beginning photography skills.

John Petek with man size Cinnamon rolls

Breakfast Pizza

handwritten recipe card from Connie Petek Hendrix

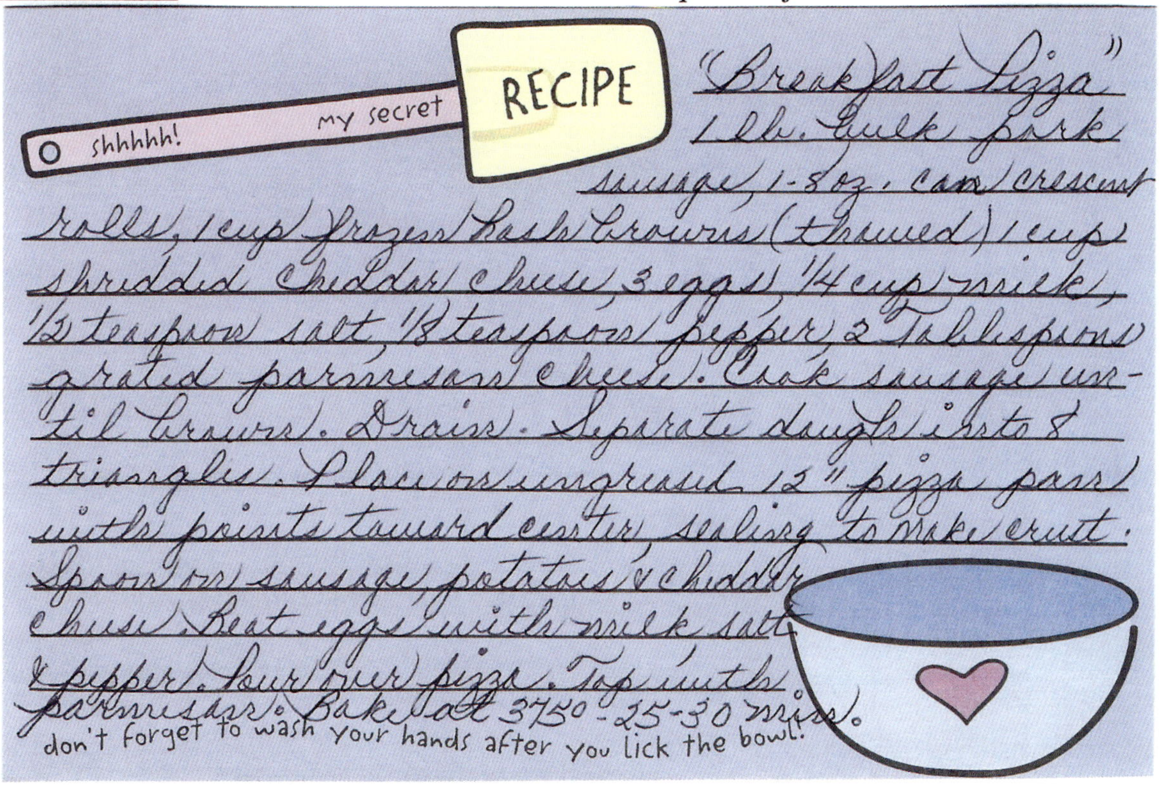

"Breakfast Pizza"
1 lb. bulk pork sausage, 1-8 oz. can crescent rolls, 1 cup frozen hash browns (thawed) 1 cup shredded Cheddar cheese, 3 eggs, 1/4 cup milk, 1/2 teaspoon salt 1/8 teaspoon pepper 2 Tablespoons grated parmesan cheese. Cook sausage until brown. Drain. Separate dough into 8 triangles. Place on ungreased 12" pizza pan with points toward center sealing to make crust. Spoon on sausage potatoes & cheddar cheese. Beat eggs with milk salt & pepper. Pour over pizza. Top with parmesan. Bake at 375° - 25-30 mins.

Cinnamon Roll Waffles with Creamy Maple Glaze

1 roll refrigerated cinnamon rolls with cream cheese frosting (the small ones)
½ cup powdered sugar **¼ cup milk** **¼ cup real maple syrup**

Preheat waffle iron; open cinnamon rolls and remove frosting. In small bowl, whisk together frosting, milk, powdered sugar, and maple syrup until smooth; set aside. Spray waffle iron with cooking spray; set cinnamon rolls on waffle iron and press down, cooking for 4 to 5 minutes until cooked. Serve with glaze.

Before Bob McClure took over the Texaco gas station, John Petek ran it with the help of June and his daughters, Connie and Cathie. Those little girls were pretty busy in that neighborhood and could make a game out of most anything they were doing. They used to pretend they were rock and roll music stars and used the gas pump nozzles for their microphones. When they were tired of that adventure, they would go over to the Perkle house where Olga always had some kind of homemade goodies to feed the kids in her household and the neighborhood.

The Perkle house, built about 1920

The home of Olga and Edward "Spike" Perkle was a hot spot for kids to gather after school and during cold days. The house was originally located across the highway from Lambkin's Bar and Café and adjacent to our ice-skating rink before the Texaco station was built. The house was later moved so the Lincoln Bank could be built on that spot. The house was relocated behind the Bootlegger Bar.

The bank that was built where the Perkle home once stood, with the Texaco and John Petek's shop in the background

Olga Perkle

YOU'RE A STAR

Children would go to the Perkle house to warm up while ice skating or just to see what was cooking in Olga's kitchen. The story goes that whenever Olga would bake cinnamon rolls, donuts or cookies, there would be a stream of town kids going in the front door, marching through the kitchen, and then exiting out the back door munching on some form of sweet treat. There was a worn path through the trees from the Perkle house to Stoner's Store, as Cathie Petek spent many hours at the Perkle home. Olga was considered a "second mother" by many children and always seemed to enjoy the crowd of kids at her home.

Olga and Spike were each married before. After their spouses died, they met and were married in Butte in 1949. Olga's children, Eileen and Dale Salmon, and Spike's son, Eddy, moved into the family home on Main Street. The Perkles later had children of their own. Spike worked in the mines, tended bar and was known for his homemade wines and cooking skills, especially with deer and elk meat.

Olga Perkle's specialty was pasties. Just imagine if John Petek and Olga Perkle would have combined their interests and formed the "Petek and Perkle Pancake, Pastries and Pasties Pub." Connie and Cathie loved to watch and help Olga in her kitchen. Today there is such a fascination with cooking shows on TV, but in our day we got to see adults in real life showing us about cooking.

Olga was active in the Lincoln PTA. She helped organize many programs and parties for children that were held at the school and community hall. There were always games and great treats at the parties, and the cookies were the best.

First-Prize Doughnuts

2 pkgs. or 2 Tbsp. active dry yeast
½ cup warm milk (110 to 115 degrees)
½ cup shortening
2 eggs
4½ to 5 cups flour
½ cup warm water (110 to 115 degrees)
½ cup sugar
1 tsp. salt
Oil for deep-fat frying

Toppings: **1¼ cups powdered sugar** **4 to 6 Tbsp. water** **Colored sprinkles**

In a large bowl, dissolve yeast in warm water. Add the milk, sugar, shortening, eggs, salt and 2 cups flour; beat until smooth. Stir in enough remaining flour to form a soft dough.

Turn onto a floured surface; knead until smooth and elastic, about 6 to 8 minutes. Place in a greased bowl, turning once to grease the top. Cover and let rise in warm place until doubled, about 1 hour.

Punch dough down. Turn onto a floured surface; roll out to ½ inch thickness. Cut with a floured 2½ inch doughnut cutter. Place on greased baking sheets. Cover and let rise until doubled.

In an electric skillet or deep-fat fryer, heat oil to 375 degrees. Fry doughnuts, a few at a time, until golden brown, on both sides. Drain on paper towels. In a shallow bowl, combine the powdered sugar and water until smooth. Dip the warm doughnuts in the glaze; decorate as desired with sprinkles.

Olga's Cocoa Roll

Lincoln Cookbook

5 egg yolks and 5 egg whites (beaten separately)
3 Tbsp. cocoa
½ cup powdered sugar
¼ tsp. salt
1 tsp. vanilla extract

Beat egg yolks until thick and frothy; add powdered sugar, cocoa, salt and vanilla. Fold in stiffly beaten egg whites last and pour into a buttered jelly roll pan or one about 9 x 14-inches, lined with waxed paper. Bake for 30 minutes at 350 degrees. Remove from pan to a damp cloth, roll up and let it cool. When cooled, unroll, spread with sweetened whipped cream and reroll. Dust with powdered sugar. Allow to stand for some time before slicing to serve.

Blue Ribbon Cinnamon Rolls

2 pkgs. active dry yeast
¼ cup shortening
2 eggs
3 cups lukewarm water
¾ cup sugar
10 cups sifted flour
½ cup butter or margarine
2 tsp. salt

Topping: **1 cup brown sugar** **1 cup maple flavored syrup** **½ cup butter or margarine**

Filling: **melted butter or margarine, sugar and ground cinnamon**

Sprinkle yeast on lukewarm water; stir to dissolve. Add ½ cup melted butter, shortening, sugar, salt, eggs and 2 cups flour. Beat with electric mixer at medium speed until smooth. Gradually add remaining flour to make soft dough that leaves the sides of the bowl using a dough hook on the mixer. *(I can't add all the flour with my old mixer, so I add about 6 more cups and then pour the dough out onto the remaining flour and knead the rest in.)* Place dough in lightly greased bowl; turn over to grease top. Cover and let rise in warm place until doubled, about 1½ hours.

Combine syrup, ½ cup butter and brown sugar in saucepan. Heat until sugar dissolves stirring occasionally. Remove from heat. Cool to lukewarm. Pour syrup mixture evenly into two 9 x 13-inch baking pans. Divide dough in half. Roll each into 12 x 14-inch rectangle on floured surface. Spread with melted butter. Sprinkle with cinnamon and sugar. Roll up like a jelly roll from narrow side. Cut into 12 slices. Place in prepared pan. Repeat with remaining dough half. Let rise until doubled, about 45 minutes. Bake in 375 degree oven 30 minutes. Immediately flip pan onto a wax paper lined large cookie sheet to easily remove the rolls and let them cool. Makes 24 rolls.

Olga also helped organize the community picnic held each year at Hooper Park on the last day of school. Each mother made her specialty dish and prepared enough for the whole community, as the men would also attend the picnic which was a grand feast. Olga made her famous potato salad in a bowl the size of a washtub and brought plenty of her famous dill pickles.

One of Olga's greatest contributions was described in the *Great Falls Tribune* in 2007, written by Kim Skornogoski in the following article:

"87-year-old woman makes pasties to save building"

Olga Perkle and a crew of cooks prepared hundreds of pasties, earning a pretty penny to repair the aging community hall in Lincoln.

Sitting in the center of town, the barn-red, octagonal log building has been used for community gatherings from public meetings and elections to family reunions, weddings and funerals since it was constructed in 1918. It's even served as the school and a roller rink at different times.

The building was constructed using donations, including the land, which was given to the community by Len Lambkin.

So naturally when the need came to replace some of the 10-inch logs, the community stepped up to raise the $10,000 needed to qualify for some $60,000 in federal grants.

Perkle came up with the idea to sell pasties, using donations of $50 and $100 from her two granddaughters for seed money to buy the hamburger, carrots, potatoes and spices to make the traditional treats from Cornwall, England.

The 87-year-old picked up her recipe living in Butte, before she moved to Lincoln in 1949. She and eight other cooks spent seven hours assembling the ingredients inside pie crust and baking 170 pasties over one weekend. The pasties were gone in a day, with orders for 60 more.

Perkle said within a few months, the women were able to raise half of the needed money. Businesses and clubs donated cash, and other groups raised money through raffles to come up with the remainder.

People purchased extra hamburger during their grocery trips and donated it, so more pasties could be prepared. "We could hardly get them out of the oven fast enough before we sold them," she said. "I think now, we've created a monster. We have so many orders."

At first she tried to keep track of how many they made, but soon got caught up in just making them fast enough.

Though they've reached their fundraising goal, Perkle is planning to cook more pasties in January to raise a little extra cash to cover any unforeseen expenses with the project and to meet the public demand.

"It's been a fun venture," she said.

Pasties

Olga Perkle
Old Lincoln Cookbook

Use coarsely **ground meat, beef or wild meat.** Use as much or a little more **potatoes,** cubed into ½ or ¼ inch cubes, **onion,** sliced to suit taste, a little **carrot, diced and parsley.** Season with **salt and pepper.** If using wild meat, use more cooking oil. Mix thoroughly and place about a cupful into **rich pastry dough.** Fold dough over and place in pan. Cut slits on top, bake in moderate oven for 1 hour.

Bacon and Egg Breakfast Pizza

1 envelope quick-rise yeast
1 tsp. sugar
½ tsp. salt
1½ cups flour
½ cup water
1 Tbsp. vegetable oil
1 Tbsp. cornmeal

In a large bowl, combine the yeast, sugar, salt and ¾ cup flour; set aside. In a small saucepan, heat water and oil to 120 degrees; stir into dry ingredients. Stir in enough remaining flour to form soft dough (it will be sticky).Turn onto a floured surface; knead until smooth and elastic, about 6 to 8 minutes. Place in a greased bowl, turning once to grease the top. Cover with plastic wrap and let rise for 10 minutes. Grease a 14-inch pizza pan; sprinkle with cornmeal. Roll out and transfer dough to prepared pan; build up edges slightly. Bake at 400 degrees for 13-15 minutes, or until edges are lightly browned.

Toppings:

1 Tbsp. butter
4 eggs
¼ tsp. salt
Dash pepper
¼ cup onion and green pepper are optional
¾ cup salsa
½ pound Canadian bacon, chopped
4 bacon strips, cooked and crumbled
1¼ cups mozzarella cheese, shredded

In a small skillet, melt butter over medium heat. Whisk eggs, salt and pepper; add to skillet. Cook and stir until just set. Spread salsa over pizza crust layer with meats, egg mixture and cheese. Bake 5 to 6 minutes longer or until cheese is melted.

Cherry Almond Streusel Scones

2 cups flour
6 Tbsp. sugar
¼ tsp. salt
2 tsp. baking powder
6 Tbsp. cold butter, cubed
1 egg
¾ cup heavy whipping cream
½ tsp. almond extract
¼ cup dried cherries

Streusel:

2 Tbsp. flour
2 Tbsp. brown sugar
¼ tsp. ground cinnamon
Pinch salt
1 Tbsp. cold butter
2 Tbsp. sliced almonds

In a large bowl, combine the flour, sugar, baking powder and salt. Cut in butter until mixture resembles coarse crumbs. Whisk the cream, egg and extract; stir into crumb mixture just until moistened. Stir in cherries. Transfer to a greased baking sheet. Pat into an 8-inch circle. Cut into eight wedges, but do not separate. For streusel, combine the flour, brown sugar, cinnamon and salt; cut in the butter until crumbly. Stir in almonds. Sprinkle over dough. Bake at 400 degrees for 20 to 25 minutes until brown.

French Toast Bake

1 loaf sourdough bread
2 Tbsp. vanilla extract
8 eggs
½ cup heavy cream
2 cups milk
¾ cup sugar

Topping:

½ cup flour
½ cup brown sugar
¼ tsp. salt
1 tsp. cinnamon
½ cup cold butter, cut in pieces

Cut loaf into cubes and place evenly in a greased 9 x 13-inch pan. In a bowl, mix eggs, milk, cream, sugar and vanilla. Pour evenly over bread. Cover pan with plastic wrap and refrigerate overnight. Mix the dry topping ingredients in a bowl; then cut in butter with mixture until crumbly and place in a baggie and refrigerate overnight as well. In morning, take pan and baggie out when ready to bake and sprinkle crumb mixture evenly over the bread. Bake at 350 degrees for 45 minutes to 1 hour for desired softness.

Another great lady from Lincoln's past was Juna McClure. Juna excelled at many things, one of which was the birthday parties she gave for her son Bobby. Most people call him Bob nowadays, except those of us who have known him since he was six years old.

Juna made Bobby's birthday parties such a fun time for everyone. Like June Petek's parties, there was lots of cake and ice cream and games. The difference was that there were boys at Bobby's parties; therefore, the games would become quite competitive. There would be different teams playing many types of relay games for really neat prizes.

Juna always made the same chocolate cake recipe for Bobby's parties, which is also in *The Lincoln Cookbook.* She would hide coins (clean of course) in the cake batter before baking the cake. (OSHA would probably object to that practice now days.) Nobody ever choked in our little group though, as we were too busy trying to find those coins in our cake before eating it. And if anybody had ever happened to choke at one of our little soirees I am sure those boys would have figured out some sort of rough and tumble Heimlich maneuver to show us girls how strong and prepared they were.

Pictured from bottom left to right at one of Bobby McClure's February 8th Birthday parties are: Butch Gehring with the top of his head showing, David Rittenhaler, Claudia Wildin, Bobby McClure, Terry Routzahn, Stacy McClure (baby), Steve Welch, Karleen Hammer, Bobby Lantis, Diana Welch, Norman and Mary Grosfield.

Our friend Diana remembers how great Juna's cakes were. Diana used the same chocolate cake recipe for her children's parties when they were growing up. (See the next page for Juna and Diana's recipe.) Diana says this recipe makes a three-layer cake. She says she usually makes two layers and uses the rest of the batter for cupcakes. Diana always preferred to make this cake for her boys, since chocolate and boys just naturally go together. This sounds like my formula for a mess which is:
Mess = boys/chocolate cake x dirt/grease.)

Another of Juna's talents was decorating her home to make it warm and cozy. I especially liked going to Juna's house because it was the same little house that my parents rented one summer before we moved to Lincoln. We lived there while my father was building summer homes and cabins back in the early 1950s. I always thought that house was somewhat plain and dreary when we lived there. That little house took on a whole new personality when the McClures bought it and fixed it up so nicely. It is amazing what cute curtains, rugs, lamps, plants, knickknacks and wall hangings can do to brighten up a house.

Juna's flair for homemaking and decorating was matched by her gifts for cooking and entertaining. She also loved children and animals, as seen in the photo of Bob's baby sister, Stacey and his dog, Babe.

Juna's Chocolate Cake

Juna McClure
Old Lincoln Cookbook

1 cup shortening
2 cups sugar
2 eggs
2 tsp. baking soda in 1 cup hot water
3 cups flour, unsifted
6 tbsp. cocoa, more or less for how dark you want it
1 cup buttermilk

Beat shortening and sugar together. Add and beat in the eggs. Sift flour and cocoa together. Add flour alternately with soda - water and buttermilk
Bake in three layer pans for about 30 minutes at 350 degrees.

Creamy White Icing

a favorite recipe of Evelyn Hammer Young from *Betty Crocker's Cookbook*

Melt **½ cup butter** in a saucepan: Remove from heat and blend in **2½ Tbsp. flour and ¼ tsp. salt.** Slowly stir in ½ **cup milk** into flour mixture then bring to a boil, stirring constantly.
Boil 1 minute then remove the white sauce base mix from heat. Stir in **3 cups sifted powdered sugar and ½ tsp. vanilla.** Beat to the right consistency. Add **½ cup chopped walnuts** if desired.

Black Devil's Food Cake

Betty Crocker's Cookbook

⅔ cup soft shortening
1⅔ cup sugar
3 eggs
⅔ cup cocoa in 1⅓ cups cold water
1 tsp. vanilla, if desired
2 cups sifted flour
⅓ tsp. baking powder
1¼ tsp. soda
1 tsp. salt

Cream shortening and sugar together until fluffy. Beat the eggs in thoroughly. Sift the dry ingredients and blend in alternately with the cocoa-water mixture. Add vanilla.
Bake in two greased and floured 9-inch cake pans at 350 degrees for 30-35 minutes.
Bake 35-45 minutes for a 9 x 13-inch pan.

Rocky Road Oatmeal Cookie Bars

Cookie Crust:
⅓ cup butter, softened
2 eggs
1 cup flour
½ tsp. salt
1 cup brown sugar
½ tsp. vanilla
1 tsp. baking soda
3 cups old fashioned oats

Topping:
1 cup mini marshmallows
⅔ cup chocolate chips
⅓ cup walnuts

Preheat oven to 350 degrees and lightly grease a 9 x 13-inch baking pan.
Beat butter and brown sugar in a large bowl until light and fluffy. Add the eggs, one at a time, beating until combined. Beat in the vanilla. Sift the flour, baking soda and salt and mix in on low speed. Add the oatmeal and mix in on low speed as well, until just combined.
Spread evenly in the baking pan. Bake for 20 minutes. Combine the topping ingredients and spread them over the cookie bar. Bake for another 10 to 13 minutes.

The house wasn't the only thing that the McClures changed. They bought the corner lot on Highway 89 (now 200) and Stemple Road, which was our ice-skating rink. We lost our skating rink but gained a new Texaco station in its place. Juna helped to run the full-service station while Bob Sr. ran the mechanical and tire portions of the station and the wrecker.

The photo shows the empty lot and the Perkle house with George Stoner's newly purchased large underground fuel tank for the upcoming Texaco station on the right. John Petek's shop is on the left in the photo and is still there. The Perkle house was moved to make room for the bank.

Juna McClure

The picture below shows the new Texaco station. The empty lot to the left is where Pat Mulcare later built another gas station. That gas station was recently demolished and the lot was empty again, but not for long. A new bank is there now, and the Texaco station is now an arts center.

McCLURE'S TEXACO

Bobby McClure and Butch Gehring were the best of friends. Bobby's family usually made sure to include Butch in many of their family and community events.

Juna served as a Boy Scout leader and was able to take Butch and the other boys under her wing and made them all feel special.

My husband became close friends with Bobby and Butch when they stayed in Augusta for high school. They spent many hours helping with mechanical work on vehicles of various varieties after school with my future husband in his father's shop. Bobby was also the best man at our wedding back in 1967, while Butch was off in the service by then.

Bob McClure

Clifford Gehring

Art Smith

Chocolate Sheet Cake *Lincoln Cookbook*

1 stick margarine **½ cup shortening** **4 Tbsp. cocoa**
1 cup water Combine these 4 ingredients in a saucepan and bring to a rapid boil.
2 cups sugar **2 cups flour** Sift together into a large bowl.
Add hot shortening mixture and beat well. Then add:
½ cup buttermilk **2 eggs** **1 tsp. soda**
1 tsp. cinnamon **1 tsp. vanilla**

Mix well and pour into a greased 11 x 16 x1-inch pan. Bake at 350 degrees for 20 to 25 minutes. Test as usual for doneness (when a toothpick inserted into middle comes out clean and dry). While cake is baking, mix icing. I use the same saucepan for frosting that I melted the shortening in.

Chocolate Frosting

Mix and bring to a boil in a saucepan:
1 stick margarine **4 Tbsp. cocoa** **6 Tbsp. milk**

Remove from heat and pour over **1 pound powdered sugar.** Beat well and add **1 tsp. vanilla.** Beat and add **1 cup coarsely chopped walnuts.** Spread over warm cake.

Juna used buttermilk in several of her recipes. There is powdered buttermilk out there, but it can be expensive and doesn't keep very well. I buy a quart of buttermilk in order to make cakes and then use the rest in a ranch salad dressing. One can also use regular milk with a tablespoon of vinegar; let it sit a while to sour and substitute it for the buttermilk.

Devil's Food Layer Cake *Country Fair Cookbook*

1 cup sugar **1 egg, slightly beaten** **¾ cup cocoa**
1 cup milk

Sift together sugar and cocoa into a heavy 2-qt. saucepan. Stir in the egg, then gradually stir in the cup of milk. Cook over medium heat, stirring constantly, until mixture coats a spoon. Remove from heat; cool completely.

¾ cup butter or margarine **1 cup sugar** **2 eggs**
½ cup milk **2 cups sifted cake flour (see below)**
1 tsp. baking soda **¼ tsp. salt**

Sift together dry ingredients. Cream together butter and 1 cup sugar until light and fluffy. Add the 2 eggs, one at a time, beating well after each addition. Beat in cooled chocolate mixture. Add dry ingredients alternately with ½ cup milk, beating well after each addition. Pour batter into 2 greased and floured 9-inch round cake pans. Bake in a 350 degree oven 25 to 30 minutes or until cakes test done. Cool in pans on racks 10 minutes. Remove from pans; cool on racks. Frost with your favorite frosting.

To make cake flour – Place 2 Tbsp. cornstarch in a 1-cup measuring cup. Fill cup with all-purpose flour and sift 3 times. Mixture is equal to 1 cup of sifted cake flour.

The McClures had two more children, Stacey and Brian, who were quite a bit younger than Bobby and our group. The McClures took in another child, Art Smith, and cared for him like he was their own. He came to live with the McClures when he was about twelve years old and attended grade school with us in Lincoln and high school in Augusta. He was quite the class clown and kept us laughing with his stunts.

Then, what all women fear the most, Bob Sr. died suddenly from a heart attack at the young age of forty-seven years old. Juna was left alone to raise and care for four children, and to run the home and the station. Bobby helped Juna manage the service station for several years after Bob Sr. died.

Juna later moved to Missoula and worked for several years at the Hallmark store in the mall. I used to enjoy seeing her there whenever we were in Missoula shopping or visiting my daughters when they were in college. Juna was still in Missoula when she died in 2007. She was a remarkable and hardworking woman, who handled the loss of her husband and later her daughter, Stacey, with grace and dignity. Juna loved to laugh and had as much fun at birthday parties as we did. She was always respectful, loving and caring toward all.

Proverbs 31: 15-18 A truly good wife "gets up before dawn to prepare breakfast for her family, and plans the day's work for her household. She goes out to inspect a field, and buys it; with her own hands she plants a vineyard. She is energetic, a hard worker, and watches for bargains."

Lessons learned from Juna's life: Marriage is not like the fairy tales where everyone lives happily ever after. Through death, divorce disease, and/or dysfunction, a man may leave physically and/or emotionally. It is best for a woman to know how to run a business or earn a living, to work hard, to care for others and to be able to carry on alone should the unforeseen happen.

An old photo shows Bob McClure Sr. riding in the Lincoln rodeo in 1950.

Bobby's grandson Kody is already quite a cowboy at a young age. He has mastered sheep riding events and is now learning to ride wild steers on his way up to the bulls.

Athletic skills come easily to the children of the McClure family. Bobby could outrun most anybody during our grade school and high school years.

Once Bobby was able to drive though, it was cars and working on them that became his passion.

Bobby and my husband still remain best of friends. It is so fun to listen as they reminisce about the pranks they used to pull during their Augusta high school years.

Kody Gunderson

Picture of Bob Sr. with his dog and nephew about 1950.
Bob Jr. is pictured in a recent photo with his dogs, Swede and Smooch.

Dirt Dessert

1 (16oz.) pkg. Oreo cookies
1 cup sugar
8 oz. Cool Whip
2 (3oz.) pkg. instant milk chocolate pudding
½ cup Bailey's Irish Cream
8 oz. cream cheese
¾ cup margarine
2½ cups milk

Variation: Can omit Bailey's Irish Cream; increase milk to 3 cups instead

Crush Oreos in blender or food processor; set aside. Mix together cream cheese, margarine, sugar and Cool Whip. In mixer blend chocolate pudding, milk, and Irish Cream. Stir pudding and cream cheese mixture together. Layer half of Oreo mixture in bottom of a clear bowl; pour in pudding mixture and top with remaining Oreo crumbs. Refrigerate until ready to use. To serve, spoon into bowls.

Rocky Road Bars

1 cup pecans, chopped
1 cup butter
½ cup cocoa
¾ tsp. salt
1 (4 oz.) semisweet chocolate baking bar, chopped
2 cups sugar
4 large eggs
1 (10.5 oz.) bag miniature marshmallows
1½ cups flour
1 tsp. vanilla

Place pecans in a single layer on a baking sheet. Bake at 350 degrees for 8 to 10 minutes until toasted. Microwave 1 cup butter and semisweet chocolate in a large microwave-safe glass bowl on HIGH for 1 minute or until melted and smooth, stirring every 30 seconds.

Whisk sugar, cocoa, egg, salt, flour and vanilla into chocolate mixture. Pour batter into a greased 15 x 10 x 1-inch jelly-roll pan. Bake at 350 degrees for 20 minutes. Remove from oven and sprinkle evenly with miniature marshmallows; bake 8 to 10 more minutes or until golden brown. Drizzle warm cake with Chocolate Frosting (recipe below), and sprinkle evenly **with toasted pecans or walnuts.**

Chocolate Frosting

½ cup butter
1 (16 oz.) pkg. powdered sugar
⅓ cup cocoa
1 tsp. vanilla
⅓ cup milk

Stir together butter, cocoa and milk in a medium saucepan over medium heat until butter is melted. Cook, stirring constantly, 2 minutes or until slightly thickened; remove from heat. Beat in powdered sugar and vanilla at medium-high speed with an electric mixer until smooth.

There is no difference between powdered sugar and confectioners' sugar

Mudd Cake

2 cups sugar
1 cup cooking oil
2 tsp. baking soda
1 cup cocoa
2 eggs
1 cup warm water
¼ tsp. salt
1 tsp. vanilla
2¼ cups sifted flour

Combine sugar, cocoa, salt and oil in bowl; beat until well blended. Add eggs, one at a time, beating well after each addition. Beat in vanilla. Combine baking soda and water. Add flour to cocoa mixture alternately with soda mixture, beating well after each addition. Pour batter into greased and floured 13 x 9 x 2-inch baking pan.

Bake at 350 degrees for 45 minutes or until cake test done. Cool in pan on rack 15 minutes. Remove from pan, if desired; cool on rack.

Frost with Muddy Chocolate Frosting: Combine **3 Tbsp. butter and ⅓ cup milk** in 2-qt. saucepan. Heat until butter melts. Remove from heat. Sift together **3 cups powdered sugar and ½ cup cocoa.** Stir into hot mixture; beat until smooth. Beat in **1 tsp. vanilla**. Spread quickly on cooled cake.

To substitute baking cocoa for baking chocolate in recipes: 1 Tbsp. of shortening or oil plus 3 level Tbsp. of cocoa may be substituted for 1 square (1 oz.) unsweetened baking chocolate.

Pauline and Leonard Orr moved to Lincoln in 1943 and were caretakers at the 7-Up Ranch some five miles east of Lincoln. My father had known Leonard previously from the Belt area where they grew up. The Orrs loved Lincoln and once invited my father and mother to come up for a visit. My dad fell in love with the Lincoln area and vowed to my mother that Lincoln was where they would be headed as soon as he could find a way to make a living.

When Dad got his first building job in Lincoln, we were neighbors with the Orrs on Eighth Avenue. Their house was located on the corner of C Street and Eighth Avenue. There weren't many other houses in that area then except for the Dan Lantis house, a little farther west on C Street, and the Wells place on Eighth Avenue. A log cabin owned by the Scotts was also in that block and is still standing in very good shape to this day. We rented the house that Bob and Juna McClure later bought.

The Orrs were our first friends and neighbors and helped my parents get settled in the community. Their youngest son, Jimmy, was my sister's age and they became good friends and could find all kinds of adventures. Betty Jean was a few years older than Donna and me, but she still played with us quite often. We were often invited over to the Wells house to play with Phyllis in her playhouse. I thought that playhouse was the neatest thing I had ever seen and I always wanted to be over there. Bob Orr was a teenager then and we never saw much of him. Since Bob was older, he never got involved in the nonsense things that the rest of us did. Bob did work for the Peteks when they ran Stoner's Store and helped deliver groceries to those who couldn't get out to shop. Bob is involved in many Lincoln activities even after his retirement from the Lincoln Phone Company some years back.

Pauline Orr became another one of those role model mothers from my early years of growing up in Lincoln. She was featured in the *Blackfoot Valley Dispatch* in the November 28, 2008, issue titled, *Montana Pioneer to Celebrate Her 90th Birthday.* The article tells about Pauline growing up and homesteading in Malta, Montana, and her early years in Lincoln after marrying husband Leonard in 1937. "Pauline worked in Stoner's Store, which also had a lunch counter and the telephone switch board. The Stoner's operated the grocery store, garage and the Lincoln Stage Line in addition to the local telephone company." The article also described many of the activities Pauline was involved with in Lincoln, such as the Cub Scouts and Boy Scouts.

Betty Jean was a very good friend while growing up in Lincoln. She loved animals and outdoor activities. She and my sister Donna were horse lovers and spent many hours riding horses as kids. In fact, they were fascinated with horses and rode them even through their teen years. My mother and Pauline would take turns driving us to the 7-Up Ranch where we could rent gentle "dude" horses when we first started riding, and for 50 cents we could ride all around that area for most of a day. I didn't have a picture of Betty Jean riding a horse, but I got a Christmas card from June Petek many years ago with a girl ice-skating that reminded me of Betty Jean with her love of the outdoors and animals. I had hoped to use that card but couldn't due to copyright issues.

Pauline also did some adventurous activities with us girls as well as the boys. She was often the one driving the truck when we went on toboggan rides over some rough terrain. She liked the Sucker Creek Road area and would hot rod on the road and in the fields along the road to give us quite a thrilling ride.

Only my dad could come close to her driving skills when it came to fast and crazy rides. She once got a buy on a sled that had some problems with

Homemade Candies

my favorite recipe!

Divinity

1¾ cups sugar
½ cup corn syrup
½ cup water
½ tsp. white vinegar

Stir until sugar is dissolved; then cook without stirring to hard ball stage (252 degrees). Remove from the heat and pour, beating constantly with an electric mixer, into: **2 egg whites, stiffly beaten** in the mixing bowl. Continue beating until mixture holds its shape and loses its shiny gloss. Add: **1 tsp. vanilla and ½ cup broken nuts.** Drop quickly from the tip of spoon onto waxed paper for individual candies, or spread in a greased shallow pan and cut into 1-inch squares when firm.

Almond Roca

2 cups butter
2 cups sugar
3 Tbsp. water
2 Tbsp. light corn syrup
Dash of salt
1 cup finally chopped almonds
1½ cups finely chopped walnuts
1 pkg. (12 oz.) semi sweet or milk chocolate chips

Melt butter over low heat in a 4-quart heavy saucepan; add sugar, water, corn syrup and salt and stir until sugar dissolves. Then cook over low heat without stirring until 290 degrees on candy thermometer. Remove from heat and stir in 1 cup almonds. Spread on buttered cookie sheet (with sides). Let stand until cool. Remove to waxed paper. Melt ½ of chocolate chips and spread on candy. Sprinkle with ½ (¾ cup) of walnuts. Let stand until chocolate is hard. Turnover and do the other side with rest of chocolate and nuts. When hard, break into small pieces.

Fudge

3 cups sugar
⅔ cup evaporated milk
¾ cup margarine
1 tsp. vanilla extract
1 (12 oz.) pkg. semi-sweet chocolate chips
1 (7oz.) jar marshmallow crème
1 cup chopped nuts

Combine sugar, margarine and milk. Bring to boil. Boil for 5 minutes or until 234 degrees on candy thermometer. Add chocolate chips and marshmallow creme and stir to melt and blend in. Add walnuts and vanilla. Pour into a 9 x 13-inch pan and cool.

Candied Nuts

1 cup sugar
¾ cup hot water
1 tsp. cinnamon
¼ tsp. cream of tartar

Put all ingredients into a frying pan. Cook until it forms a soft ball stage (fairly firm). Stir often. Take from burner and add: **1 tsp. vanilla and 2 to 3 cups walnuts or almonds.** Stir until sugary and nuts are covered. Spread out on wax paper and separate.

Chocolate Caramels *Lincoln Cookbook*

2 cups sugar
2 squares chocolate
1 tsp. vanilla extract
1 cup light cream
½ cup light corn syrup
1½ cup pecans, chopped
1 cup butter
½ tsp. salt

Combine all but vanilla and nuts in a large saucepan. Bring to boil over low heat. Cook until firm ball stage (248 degrees). Cool 5 minutes. Stir in vanilla and nuts. Pour into 8 x 8-inch pan.

ground, but we sat a few feet up above the runners. It was like a small, skinny sleigh, but only wide enough for one person and not much longer. We were able to get three little girls on it anyway. It didn't take long to discover a big flaw in its design. That thing kept tipping over even with careful driving on Pauline's part and us sitting as still as we could. We spent all our time and energy putting it back upright and climbing back on to try again and again to stay on top of the snow instead of buried in it. Pauline would take us back to her house to dry off and warm up. We would have hot chocolate and homemade treats. Her candy and cookies were the best.

I always loved to stop by and see Pauline on some of my trips to Lincoln. My husband and I used to stop by at Christmas time and Pauline would always send us home with homemade candy and goodies. Divinity (my favorite) was her specialty. Visiting with Pauline is always so fun as she is so easygoing, cheerful and happy. I love to hear her deep laugh and funny stories.

I remember Leonard Orr as a very kind and quiet man who would just shake his head and chuckle over Pauline's silly antics and stories.

Another Christmas card from June Petek that reminded me of "the good old days in Lincoln"

I didn't find any of Pauline's recipes in the original Lincoln Cookbook, so I substituted other recipes for those that I remember Pauline used to make.

Chocolate Covered Candies

Some handy tips from *Taste of Home Christmas Cookies and Candies Cookbook (2008)* are:

- When making chocolate-dipped candies, combine the chocolate with shortening—don't be tempted to substitute margarine. Margarine contains water, which will cause chocolate to "seize" or curdle, so it can't be used to dip or coat candies. (p. 64)
- When chocolate candy is stored at temperatures in the upper 70s and higher, white streaks or dots may develop. To prevent this, chocolate that contains cocoa butter must be tempered. Tempering is the process of carefully melting and re-cooling chocolate, which allows the chocolate to stay glossy and firm. Chocolate candy coating, an ingredient in many Taste of Home candy recipes does not need to be tempered. Candy coating melts easily and maintains a smooth surface, making it a good choice for many candy recipes. (p. 62)
- Candy coating—sometimes called almond bark or confectionery coating—is available in white, milk and dark chocolate varieties. At your store, you may find large individual blocks, packages of flat disks or chips and boxes of individually wrapped 1 ounce squares. A substitute for 6 ounces of chocolate coating would be 6 ounces of chocolate chips and 1 tablespoon of shortening (Crisco) melted together. (p. 60)
- Before melting chocolate chips, be sure all equipment and utensils are completely dry. Any moisture may cause the chocolate to stiffen or "seize." Chocolate that has seized can sometimes be saved by immediately adding 1 tablespoon vegetable oil for each 6 ounces of chocolate. Slowly heat the mixture and stir until smooth. (p. 16)
- Always use a thermometer designed for candy making. It must have a movable clip that's used to secure it to the side of the pan and to keep the end of the thermometer off the bottom of the pan. Be sure to read the thermometer at eye level. A candy mixture will cook very slowly when boiling until it reaches 220 degrees, then it will cook quickly. It's important to closely watch the thermometer at this point. To avoid breakage, allow the thermometer to cool before washing it. (p. 68)
- To avoid getting unsightly white spots on your homemade chocolate candies, refrigerate them for about 10 minutes to set the chocolate—this will help keep the high gloss and firm texture you want. Then store the sweets in a cool dry place. Chocolate that comes in contact with moisture or becomes too cold during storage can develop tiny white or gray sugar crystals. Even if the crystals appear, the candy is still safe to eat. (p. 48)
- To pack candies or cookies as gifts, line your tin or decorative box with wax-coated tissue paper. You can find it at specialty cooking stores. It's sturdier than regular tissue paper and won't absorb the treat's flavor and oil. (p. 50)
- You can use a toothpick to dip round candies into melted chocolate. (p. 50)
- Always place candy balls and chocolate covered balls on waxed paper-lined baking sheets and let stand until set.
- Stored in an airtight container in a cool dry place, most homemade candy will keep for about 2 to 3 weeks. Fudge and caramels can be wrapped tightly and frozen for up to 1 year. (p. 60)

I have often wondered if Pauline was ever a snowmobile driver. Whether she was or not, her son Bob Orr was instrumental in helping to establish the Ponderosa Snow Warriors Snowmobile Club in Lincoln. Have you ever wondered how the Sucker Creek Road would become their groomed trail in the winter and why they would build their clubhouse out along that same roadway? Well I have a theory as to how it all came about. Bob Orr probably got so tired of having to dig his mother out of ditches along Sucker Creek Road with her wild sled–pulling adventures that it was just easier to organize a trail up there and hope she would stay on it.

One of Pauline's memories that was spoken about in the BVD, was that of being a Cub Scout leader with Juna McClure, and all the fun and silly adventures they had with that group of boys. Most of the boys, such as Bob McClure, Jim Orr, Steve Welch, Butch Gehring, Danny Lantis and many others, were in Cub Scouts. I can just imagine the fun those boys must have had with Pauline and Juna as leaders.

Another memory I have of Pauline and my mom was when they signed Betty Jean, Jimmy, Donna and me up for swimming lessons at the 7-Up Ranch one summer. The pool was a real cement pool, not like that portable ones of now. The present-day clearing where the second 7-Up Ranch resort stood, was where the pool and horse barns were located. This was a beautiful place to ride horses and go swim. The original 7-Up bar and restaurant were located off to the right in the trees when driving into the ranch. There is a beautiful log house there now near where the old bar and restaurant were located.

The Todds' house (they were the owners then) was to the left side of the road and is still there today. Both the new and old 7-Up Ranch resorts burned down some years back. I am not sure of the dates, but the old one was around the 1970s and the new one around 2000. I am not sure if Betty Jean, Jim or Donna ever learned to swim, but they did have fun playing in the water. I remember my mother and Pauline telling us how everyone should learn to swim just in case we were ever caught in a storm on a boat, stranded on a deserted island, falling down while wading in the river or whatever other tragedy they could think of that would require us to be able to swim in order to save a life— our own or that of someone else.

They also told of what great exercise it was and how strong we could become as we developed our arm and leg muscles from swimming. As hard as I tried, I never could get the hang of it. I tried to rationalize my inability to swim and blame it on the fact that I had polio at age five and had weak muscles. Really it was because I was afraid of the water and couldn't relax. Pauline used to tell us that if we could just relax, we would always float to the top should we ever get in over our heads.

Pauline Orr was my mom's first neighbor and friend when we moved to Lincoln. Pauline was good for my mom who was afraid of many things. My mom could always see a disaster waiting to happen, especially with all the fun adventures that Pauline was always wanting to try in order to make life fun for kids. Pauline showed us how to relax and enjoy life. She could make a party out of everyday activities. She showed others the joy of laughter and of having fun no matter what was going on.

Proverbs 14:30 "A relaxed attitude lengthens a man's/woman's life: jealousy rots it away."

To conclude: The following recipes all have different types of chocolate coatings. There are three basic recipes that one could choose to use with any of the candy recipes listed on on the following pages, which are:

1. **Chocolate candy coating (dark, white or milk)** which can be melted in a microwave oven. Work with a few frozen or cold balls of candy at a time, by dipping into the chocolate and placing them on a waxed paper-lined baking sheet. Let stand until set.
2. **2 cups (12 oz.) milk chocolate chips and 2 tablespoons shortening** can be **melted** in the microwave. Stir until smooth. Dip candy balls in the chocolate and allow excess to drip off.
3. **2 cups (12 oz.) semisweet chocolate chips, 2 packages (4 oz. each) German sweet chocolate, chopped and 2 tablespoons shortening** can be melted in a microwave. Stir until smooth. Dip balls into the chocolate mixture and allow excess to drip off.

Chocolate Covered Cherries

2½ cup powdered sugar — **¼ cup butter, softened**
1 Tbsp. milk — **½ tsp. almond extract**
2 jars (8 oz. each) maraschino cherries with stems, well drained

In a small bowl, combine the sugar, butter, milk and almond extract. Knead until smooth and pliable. Shape into 1 inch balls and flatten each into a 2 inch circle. Wrap one circle around each cherry and lightly roll in hands. Place with stems up on lined baking sheet. Cover loosely and refrigerate for 4 hours or overnight. Dip in **2 cups melted chocolate chips (milk chocolate or semi-sweet) and 2 tablespoons Crisco.** Place on waxed paper until set. Store in a covered container. Refrigerate 1 to 2 weeks before serving. Yield: 3 dozen.

Orange Coconut Creams

1 can (14 oz.) sweetened condensed milk — **½ cup butter, cubed**
1 package (2 pounds) powdered sugar — **1 cup flaked coconut**
1½ tsps. orange extract

In a small saucepan, combine milk and butter. Cook and stir over low heat until the butter is melted. Place the powdered sugar in a large bowl. Add milk mixture; beat until smooth. Add the coconut and orange extract; mix well. Roll into 1-inch balls. Place on waxed paper-lined baking sheets. Refrigerate until firm, about 1 hour. This recipe calls for the **German sweet chocolate, 2 packages (4 oz. each), semisweet chocolate chips (2 cups) and 2 tablespoons Crisco.** Dip and coat the candy. (See #3 above). Place on waxed paper after dipping; let stand until set. Yield: 9 dozen.

Chocolate Cream Bonbons

4 cups powdered sugar — **1 cup ground pecans or walnuts**
½ cup plus 2 Tbsp. sweetened condensed milk — **¼ cup butter, softened**

In a large bowl, combine the sugar, pecans, milk and butter. Roll into 1 inch balls. Place on waxed paper-lined baking sheets. Cover and refrigerate them overnight. This recipe calls for **3 cups semisweet chocolate chips and 2 tablespoons shortening;** (*I prefer milk chocolate*) Microwave and stir until smooth. Dip candies in chocolate; allow excess to drip off. Place on waxed paper. Let stand until set. Yield: about 6 dozen.

Pauline, Barbara, Mom, Millie Kenyon and me

Mom and Roy

Pauline, Millie, Mom and Barba

Happy Birthday

These photos on the top of the page were taken at my mom's (Evelyn Hammer Young) eighty-fourth birthday in August 2005 at Garland's remodeled store and sandwich shop. It was such a treat to have Pauline, Barbara Garland Solvie, Millie Kenyon Swan and my stepfather, Roy Young, as part of the birthday celebration. Garlands closed the store later that year after fifty years of serving Lincoln. I will have more about the Garlands in the next volume.

P.S. When I went to college, all freshmen had to be able to swim two laps of the pool or take beginning swimming lessons. I just signed up for class, in order to avoid any further embarrassment. I soon forgot about my fear of the water. Fear of my instructor, Miss K., soon became the biggest problem in my life. I did learn to swim but not from the screaming, drill sergeant type of teacher I had. A friend from my dorm was a lifeguard at the pool and member of the synchronized swimming team. She gave me the encouragement and help I needed to pass the class.

I enjoyed swimming so much that I signed up for an intermediate course the next quarter. I made sure I signed up with a different instructor. Well there was some kind of a snafu in the registration process, and of course I got Miss K. as my teacher again. I don't think she was any too excited about the switch around either. I soon learned that my fear of water and Miss K. weren't near as bad as my fear of diving into the deep end of the pool.

One day as we were learning to surface dive, we had to find a dime at the bottom of the deep end of the pool. I didn't get enough power in my arms to get me to the bottom of the pool; therefore I couldn't kick off the bottom to get back to the surface. I found myself fighting to connect with the side of the pool or anything I could touch to get to the top and get a breath. I knew I was drowning and trusted that Miss K would come to my rescue. I learned that when you are dying or drowning, time goes by very slowly and you can get a lot of praying, reflecting and repenting done in that time. I began to plead with God to save my life, since it didn't look like anyone else was coming to my rescue. I then remembered the advice from Pauline so many years back—*to relax and float to the top.* I finally got to the surface and saw Miss K just standing there with her arms crossed. She wasn't even yelling at me. She just stood there, probably frozen, and didn't do anything. I then remembered Pauline's advice about the strength in my arms and legs, and began using them to tread water. I believe that God and I had the situation under control when Miss K. finally handed me a pole to grab onto and pulled me back to the side of the pool. It probably occurred to her that if "that moron drowns, there goes my job." I did thank her though for saving me, just to try to ease the tension between us and make her feel like she had saved the day. Actually God with his instructions, through Pauline's advice from so long ago, is what saved my life. I just barely passed that course with a C-. I knew Miss K passed me because she was afraid that if I flunked, I would have to take the course over and she could possibly be my teacher again.

Maple Nut Chocolates

1 can (14 oz.) sweetened condensed milk
7½ cups powdered sugar
2 tsp. maple flavoring
4 cups (24 oz.) semisweet chocolate chips
2 oz. bittersweet chocolate, chopped
½ cup butter, cubed
2 cups walnuts, chopped
1 tsp. vanilla extract
2 Tbsp. shortening

In a small saucepan, combine sweetened condensed milk and butter. Cook and stir over low heat until the butter is melted. Place the powdered sugar in a large bowl; add the milk mixture and beat until smooth. Stir in the walnuts, maple flavoring and vanilla. Roll the mixture into ¾ inch balls; place on waxed paper-lined baking sheets. Refrigerate balls until firm, about 1 hour.

In a microwave, melt the chocolate chips, bittersweet chocolate and shortening; stir until smooth. Dip the balls into chocolate; allow excess to drip off. Place on waxed paper; let stand until set. Store the candy in an airtight container. Makes about 13 dozen.

Lemon Cream Bonbons

2 pkgs. (8 oz. each) cream cheese, softened
2 Tbsp. grated lemon peel
1 cup powdered sugar
3 Tbsp. lemon juice
1 tsp. lemon extract

In a large bowl, beat the cream cheese, lemon juice, peel and extract. Gradually beat in powdered sugar. Cover and freeze for 2 hours. Using a small ice cream scoop, drop mixture by 1 inch balls onto waxed paper-lined baking sheets. Cover and freeze for 1 hour. Dip ball into a chocolate coating. Let stand until firm. Drizzle white chocolate coating over the candies if desired. Store in the refrigerator. Remove just before serving. Yields 4 dozen.

Coconut Bonbons

2 cups powdered sugar
1 Tbsp. milk
½ cup butter, softened
¼ tsp. almond flavoring

Cream the above ingredients. Add; **1½ cups flaked coconut.** Mix together. Chill for 15 minutes. Form into 1 inch balls. May place an almond in center if desired. Chill for 30 minutes. Melt chocolate chips and shortening or candy coating. Dip balls in a chocolate mixture. Cool on waxed paper covered cookie sheets.

White Chocolate Peanut Butter Squares

1 Tbsp. plus ¾ cup butter, divided
⅔ cup evaporated milk
1 jar (7 oz.) marshmallow creme
1 Tbsp. vanilla extract
3 cups sugar
1 pkg. (10 oz.) peanut butter chips
1 cup nuts, chopped
1½ pound white candy coating

Line a 9 x 13-inch pan with foil. Grease the foil with 1 tbsp. butter; set aside. In a heavy saucepan, combine the sugar, evaporated milk and remaining butter (¾ cup). Bring to a boil over medium heat; cook and stir for 5 minutes. Remove from the heat; stir in the peanut butter chips until melted. Add the marshmallow creme, nuts and vanilla; stir until blended. Pour into prepared pan. Cool. Remove from pan onto waxed paper-lined baking sheets and cut into 1-inch squares. Freeze or refrigerate until firm.

In a microwave, melt candy coating (or white chocolate chips and shortening).Stir until smooth. Dip the squares into the coating. Place on waxed paper lined baking sheets until set. If desired, drizzle melted chocolate chips (½ cup) and 1 tsp. shortening over the squares. Place melted mixture in a heavy duty plastic bag. Cut a small hole in corner of bag; drizzle over candies. Store in an air-tight container. Yields 9 dozen.

Pauline Orr

Pauline (Shaver) Orr was born In Malta on Nov. 20, 1918, the only child of Elizabeth and Clinton Shaver. She grew up and went to school in Great Falls where she graduated from Great Falls High School in 1937. She was working in her mother's boarding house when she met Leonard E. Orr. They were united in marriage on July 6, 1938. They lived in Great Falls, where their first child Robert was born. A few years later their second child, Betty Jean was born and they moved to Lincoln where their third child James was born.

They raised their family in Lincoln, where they remained for the rest of their lives. Pauline worked alongside her husband in logging and also worked in sawmills, at lunch counters and in bookkeeping for the telephone company.

Pauline was separated from her husband with his death in 1992, after 54 years of marriage.

Pauline was a very kind person, a gracious hostess and a friend to all who knew her. She will be greatly missed by her family and many friends.

Pauline will be laid to rest next to her loving husband Leonard in the old Lincoln Cemetery.

She is survived by her son Robert (Myrna), his two sons Lenny and Robby and their children Jennifer and Robert;, her daughter Betty Jean (Chris) Waits; and her son James (Arlene), his two daughters, Paula and Jamie and long-time friends Kathy Orr and Pat Orr.

Article from the *Blackfoot Valley Dispatch*, 2014.

Jimmy, Betty Jean, Pauline, Leonard and Bob Orr

I received a Christmas card many years back from Mary Grosfield Sampsen with two eagles soaring above the mountaintops, which reminded me of Pauline and Leonard Orr. The inside of the card contained the famous quote from Isaiah 40:31, "*But they that wait upon the Lord shall renew their strength; they shall mount up with wings as eagles; they shall run and not be weary and they shall walk and not faint.*"

Another Bible verse that reminded me of Pauline is Nehemiah 8:10, which states, "*Do not grieve for the joy of the Lord is your strength.*" This verse reminded me of Pauline with her joy and strength to get through life. I gained a new appreciation for Pauline when Leonard died. I noticed her strength in dealing with the reality of his death, her love and concern for her family, her support for others during such a difficult time plus her strength to be able to live alone and care for herself after he was gone.

A few years back, after I became the owner of the Moffit home in Lincoln, I would take a break from painting, cleaning and yard work chores and walk over to Pauline's house for a little visit. Even after she turned ninety years old, she could still recognize me when I walked up to her house. I would find her sitting out on her porch enjoying the flowers, birds and squirrels, sunshine and life in her cute little yard.

Gumdrop Fudge

1½ pounds white candy coating, chopped
1 can (14 oz.) sweetened condensed milk
1½ cups gumdrops, chopped (not spicy)
⅛ tsp. salt **1½ tsp. vanilla**

Line a 9-inch square pan with parchment paper. In a heavy saucepan, combine the candy coating, milk and salt. Cook and stir over low heat until candy coating is melted. Remove from the heat; stir in vanilla and gumdrops. Pour into the baking pan. Cool and cut into bite sized pieces.

Microwave Peanut Brittle

1 cup light corn syrup **1 cup sugar**
1 cup water **3 Tbsp. butter**
1 pkg. raw peanuts **1 tsp. soda**
1 tsp. vanilla extract **1 tsp. water**

Mix syrup, sugar and water together and cook on full power 20 minutes. Take out and add the butter and raw peanuts. Cook for 12 more minutes. Add the soda, vanilla and water. Mix, and pour on buttered cookie sheet.

Taffy

1 cup sugar **⅔ cup water**
1 Tbsp. corn starch **¾ cup corn syrup**
1 tsp. salt **2 Tbsp. margarine**

Mix all ingredients together and boil to 250 degrees. Add flavoring and coloring before pouring into a greased pan to cool. When cool enough to handle, pull until light and brittle.

Penuche adapted from a recipe by Ruth Naughten in the *Lincoln Cookbook*

¾ cup canned milk **1 cup white sugar** **1 cup brown sugar**
¼ cup milk **1 Tbsp. corn syrup**

Put all ingredients in a heavy saucepan. Cook to soft ball stage (236 degrees); remove from heat; cool until you can hold your hand comfortably on bottom of pan. Add **2 Tbsp. butter, 2 tsp. vanilla and ½ cup chopped walnuts** if desired and beat until it loses it shine; pour into buttered pan to harden.

Petite Apricot Balls

1⅓ cups dried apricots, finally chopped **½ cup sugar**
2 tbsp. water **2 tbsp. butter** **1 tbsp. orange juice**

Place above ingredients in a heavy frying pan. Cook over medium heat, stirring until mixture becomes a thick puree. Transfer to a bowl and refrigerate for 1½ hours. Dampen hands in a little orange juice and roll small spoonful of paste into a smooth ball. *Roll in granulated or super fine* sugar *or finely chopped almonds to coat.* Put into small paper candy cups and refrigerate uncovered 2 to 3 days to allow for drying.

Caramels **(see Nellie Knights recipe on page 55)** Pauline Orr and Nellie were best of friends and neighbors when Nellie lived in Lincoln.

Snowmobiling has become one of Lincoln's most popular outdoor winter activities. Snowmobilers wait all year long for the heavy winter snows that make Lincoln such a popular area for the sport. Could Pauline's love for sledding have played a part in the development of the present snowmobile era for Lincoln? Lincoln is now becoming a popular area for snowshoeing, cross-country skiing and snowboarding as well.

Adventure in the Backcountry

A Winter Wonderland of Snowshoeing or Skiing

Son-in-law Brooks Hammel with his daughter, Sydney

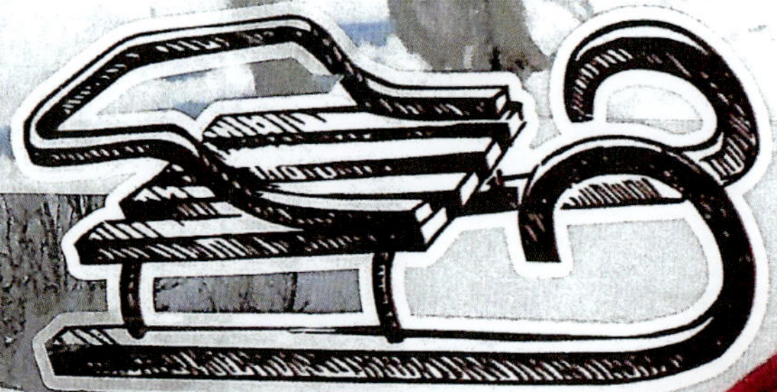

Photo by Gus Wolfe

Granddaughter Sydney Hammel

Ponderosa Snow Warriors pancake breakfast heralds snowmobile season

Bob Orr's pancakes have been a big draw to the Ponderosa Snow Warriors pancake breakfasts for around 30 years and he's glad the club was finally able to get the grill in the clubhouse repaired. For Orr, who whips up two ten-gallon buckets of pancake batter for the breakfasts, a reliable grill was no small thing as he worked to serve the folks who showed up at the clubhouse for the Snow Warriors annual welcome to winter breakfast, Dec. 8. Like many of his generation, Orr volunteers his time to help out. But there is a rising concern that such a spirit of volunteerism is lost on the younger members of the club and may impact it's ability to carry on its long list of contributions to the community and local economy.

Bob Orr flips one of his signature pancakes while Mike Nordahl takes care of the eggs at the Ponderosa Snow Warriors annual pancake breakfast. By 10 a.m the clubhouse was packed

<u>Sourdough Starter and Pancakes</u>

Janet Varland
Augusta friend

Starter: **1 cup flour** **1 cup water**
½ pkg. yeast **3 Tbsp. sugar**

Mix and put in pint jar or bowl. Let stand in warm place 12 hours.

Basic Sponge: **2 cups milk** **2½ cups flour**

Add to starter and leave in cloth covered bowl overnight in warm place. Next morning reserve 1 cup starter from basic sponge and put in covered jar in refrigerator.

Pancakes: To rest of basic sponge, add: **2 tsp. baking powder**
1 Tbsp. sugar, pinch salt, 2 eggs, and 2 tsp. soda. Beat well & fry.

PONDEROSA SNOW WARRIORS

LINCOLN, MONTANA

Bob Orr and Bob Bushnell load up a plate with pancakes and eggs at the annual Breakfast, Saturday, Dec. 7.

Despite a scarcity of snow and the bitter cold that settled over Montana last weekend, about 75 people made the trip out to the Ponderosa Snow Warriors clubhouse on Sucker Creek for their annual Pancake Breakfast to kick off the snowmobiling season.

Bob Orr, whose signature sourdough pancakes are the cornerstone of the event, said it was a little slow early on.

"I didn't know if anybody would show up when it's 25 below zero," he said. Fortunately he had pleny of pancake batter on hand, just in case.

As folks began to trickle into the clubhouse, warmed by a well-stoked fire in the stove, the building buzzed with conversations about the cold snap and the prospects for the season.

The snowmobiling season officially got underway on Dec. 1

Articles and photographs borrowed from the Blackfoot Valley Dispatch by Roger and Erin Dey

Musher Cookies by Judy Johnson

1 cup butter
6 oz. cream cheese
2 Tbsp. milk
1 egg
1 tsp. vanilla
2 cups flour
½ tsp. salt
¾ cup nuts, chopped
(Use less salt if nuts are salted)

Cream the above together then add dry ingredients. Drop by spoonfuls onto greased cookie sheets. Bake at 350 degrees for 15 to 17 minutes.

"Musher cookies have been on the Race to the Sky, Iditarod and many others. They do not freeze. Just what a musher needs on the trail......JJ"

Water color by Jim Howard

Photo by Gus Wolfe

A most amazing thing happened one February day in Lincoln while out snowmobiling. We saw Dave Armstrong mushing his sled dogs in preparation for the annual Race to the Sky event. It was one of the the most beautiful sites to behold. He and his dogs moved so swiftly and silently across the snow on a beautiful, sunny day. We were just frozen in awe as they raced out of sight after we exchanged a few shouts of support.

I have since become a big fan of the Race to the Sky event. My husband has become a collector of the Race to the Sky posters and we have some of the most beautiful ones that have been produced in the last twenty five years. Our favorite one is done by Jim Howard for the 2010 event. It isn't because he is one of our local church pastors and a close friend that impresses us. It is because his water colors are some of the most beautifully done works of art out there. What an honor to have his work chosen to represent the Race to the Sky event for that year. The 2012 winner was Judy Johnson's portrait of Dave Armstrong. See previous page for Judy Johnson's recipe for her famous Musher's cookies.

Dave Armstrong by Judy Johnson of Lincoln

Drawing by June Petek

The school years of 1955-1956 were very memorable in our little community. June Petek's talents for art, leadership, and writing became known as she assisted with two major projects that year: 1) the Christmas program and 2) "The Evergreen" school annual.

The Christmas program was a one of a kind pageant produced and directed by Mrs. Naomi (Mickie) Donaldson, our third, fourth and fifth grade teacher. Every child from our little three-room schoolhouse had some part in the production. It was called "Toyland Fantasy" and was held in the Community Hall with a packed house. The decorations and costumes were fantastic with most artwork done by June, Mickie and her husband, Bill Donaldson. The costumes were homemade with the mothers helping each other design and sew them. I don't know who did all the photography, but the pictures were great and later printed in the one and only 1955 annual, "The Evergreen." (See copies of those 1955 photos.)

MASTER OF CEREMONIES

DANNY LANTIS

DANNY

BUNNIES

TOYLAND FANTASY

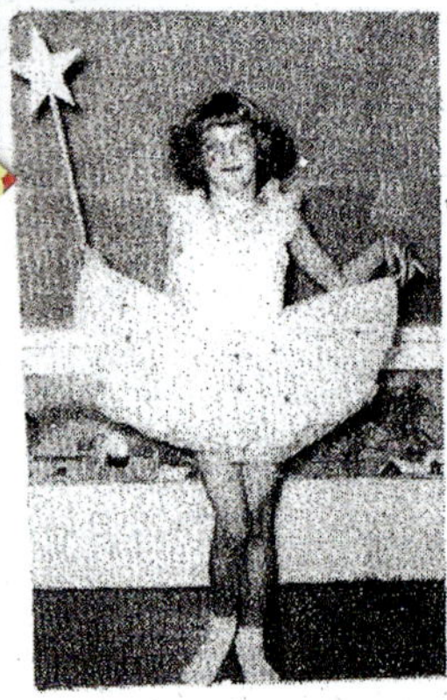

PHYLLIS

TERRY

TUMBLERS

(LEFT TO RIGHT) FRANK, DALE, MIKE PAUL, DOUG, DAVID, JOE, ERVIN, TIM, KEITH, NORMAN, EDDY (FINISHING ON BOTTOM ROW)

PENNY

CLAUDIA

CHRISTMAS COOKIES

Russian Tea Cakes

1 cup soft butter
½ cup powdered sugar, sifted
1 tsp. vanilla extract
2¼ cup flour
¼ tsp. salt
¾ cup nuts, finely chopped

Mix butter, sugar and vanilla. Stir in sifted flour and salt. Mix in nuts. Roll dough into 1 inch balls; place 2½ inches apart on ungreased baking sheet. Bake until set but not brown in 400 degrees oven 10 to 20 minutes. While still warm, roll in powdered sugar. Cool. Roll in sugar again.

Mexican Wedding Cakes

Bake same recipe as above, except **use 2 cups flour, ¼ cup powdered sugar and ¼ cup regular sugar, 2 tsp. vanilla, add ¼ tsp. cinnamon and 1 cup pecans**. Can roll warm baked cookies in red or green sprinkles for a bright color instead of powdered sugar.

Swedish Sandbakelser

⅓ cup blanched almonds
¾ cup butter or margarine
1¾ cup flour
1 egg white
¾ cup sugar

Put almonds through fine knife or food grinder twice (1 tsp. vanilla and 1 tsp. almond flavoring may be substituted for almonds). Mix in butter, sugar, and egg white thoroughly. Stir in flour. Chill.

Heat oven to 350 degrees. Press dough into sandbakelser molds (tiny fluted forms) to form thin coating. Place on ungreased baking sheet. Bake 12 to 15 minutes. Tap molds on table to loosen cookies; turn out.

Norwegian Berlinerkranser

1½ cup shortening (½ butter or margarine)
1 cup sugar
2 tsp. grated orange rind
2 eggs
4 cups flour
1 egg white
2 Tbsp. sugar
red candied cherries
green citron

Mix shortening, 1 cup sugar, rind and eggs thoroughly. Stir in sifted flour. Chill dough. Heat oven to 400 degrees. Break off small pieces of dough and roll to pencil size, about 6 inches long and ¼ inch thick. Form each piece into a circle bringing one end over and through in a single knot. Leave ½ inch end on each side. Place on ungreased baking sheet. Beat egg white until frothy; gradually beat in 2 Tbsp. sugar; brush tops with this meringue. Press bits of red candied cherries on center of knot for holly berries. Add little jagged leaves cut out of green citron. Bake 10 to 12 minutes.

Many recipes in this section are from *Betty Crocker's Picture Cookbook* (1955) and *Betty Crocker's Cooky Book* published in 1963 by General Mills Inc.

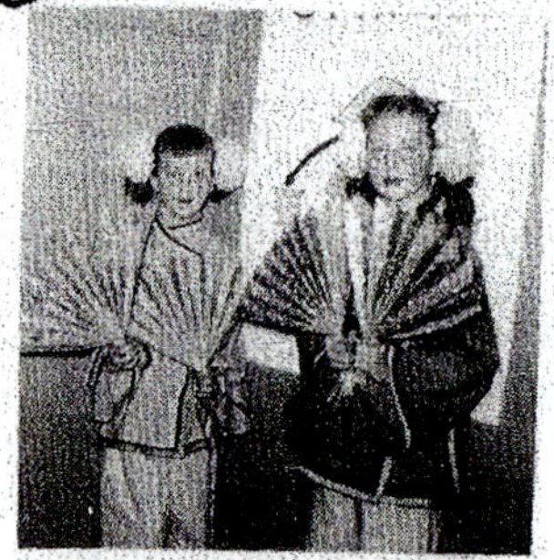

CONNIE · AND · CATHIE

LYNN · AND · DIANA

HARRY, RICHARD, TOMMY

PENNY

LINDA · AND · STEVE

BOBBY · AND · LYNN

CONNIE, PENNY, MI

SHARON + BE

MRS. DONALDSON

Scotch Shortbread *Betty Crocker's Cooky Book*

⅝ cup sugar **2½ cups flour** **1 cup butter**

Mix thoroughly with hands. Chill dough. Roll out about ½ inch thick. Cut into fancy shapes (small leaves, ovals, squares, etc.) Flute edges if desired by pinching between fingers as for pie crust. Place on ungreased baking sheet. Bake at 300 degrees for 20 to 25 minutes. (The tops do not brown during baking, nor does shape of the cookies change).

Scandinavian Krumkake

4 eggs
1 cup sugar
½ cup butter or margarine, melted
5 Tbsp. cream
¾ cup flour
2 tsp. cornstarch
1 tsp. vanilla

Heat Krumkake iron over small electric or plain gas surface unit (6 inches) on medium-high heat. Beat eggs and sugar together thoroughly; add butter, cream and vanilla. Sift and blend flour and cornstarch; stir into egg mixture. Beat until smooth. Test iron with a few drops of water; if they "jump," iron is correct temperature. Drop batter (about ½ Tbsp. for a 6 inch iron, more for larger irons) on ungreased iron; close gently—do not squeeze. Bake on each side about 15 seconds, or until light, golden brown. Keep iron over heat at all times, (Don't be alarmed if first few are dark; iron cools slightly while in use). Remove with knife; immediately roll on wooden roller.

French Lace Cookies

1 cup flour
1 cup finely chopped nuts
½ cup corn syrup
½ cup soft shortening
⅔ cup brown sugar, packed

Heat oven to 375 degrees. Blend sifted flour and nuts. Bring corn syrup, shortening and sugar to a boil in saucepan over medium heat, stirring constantly. Remove from heat; gradually stir in flour and nuts. Drop batter by level teaspoonful about 3 inches apart on lightly greased baking sheet. Bake only 8 to 9 cookies at a time, for 5 to 6 minutes. Remove from oven and allow to stand 5 minutes before removing from baking sheet. You may want to use parchment paper to help avoid cookies sticking to the pan.

Dutch Hail

1 cup butter or margarine
1 cup sugar
1 egg, separated
½ cup finely chopped walnuts
2 cups flour
½ tsp. cinnamon
1 Tbsp. water

Heat oven to 350 degrees. Lightly grease a jellyroll pan. Mix butter, sugar and egg yolk. Blend in flour and cinnamon into butter mixture. Pat into the pan. Beat water and egg white until frothy. Brush over dough; sprinkle with nuts. Bake 20 to 25 minutes or until very lightly browned. Cut immediately into finger like strips.

The annual was dedicated to Mr. Donaldson, who died during the winter of 1956. He was retired but helped his wife, Naomi (Mickie), with all her school projects, parties and programs.

I remember Mr. Donaldson because he made me a pair of angel wings to wear with my choir robe for the Christmas program. I was very shy and scared about being in the choir.

The Donaldsons invited me to their house (the little log house across from the Lincoln Community Hall) to see if a pair of wings would help me feel any better about taking part in the program. Those wings, along with the milk and cookies and the care and concern they showed for me, were all it took to get me up on stage with the rest of the choir.

We all felt such a loss when Mr. Donaldson died. He was a very quiet, kind and gentle man. He was a friend to all in our little town.

WILLIAM·(BILL)·WALDO·DONALDSON

"HE WALKS WITH ME, AND HE TALKS WITH ME..."

Now Mrs. Donaldson was another story. She was very outgoing with a voice big enough for two people. She was a very petite, dainty and classy lady. She was always beautifully dressed with the latest style, cute haircuts, jewelry and high heels. She always had shoes that matched her outfits. With her perfect posture, poise and self-confidence, she moved like a dancer in those high heels. She and June Petek were both very stylish, beautiful and well dressed. You would never catch either one of those ladies out of their house in sweats and a T-shirt, like so many dress nowadays.

Mrs. Donaldson was a dedicated teacher. The old saying about the three (3) R's (reading, writing and arithmetic) was her philosophy. Of course spelling was right upthere at the top, with a spelling bee every Friday. We spent hours practicing penmanship, working math problems on the board, conjugating verbs, diagramming sentences and, of course, reading library books, for which we were rewarded. I remember reading about eighty books while in her room. Mrs. Donaldson made school and learning a fun and exciting experience. She was always positive and upbeat. No yelling, screaming or humiliating students on her part. She gave us lots of rewards, compliments and praise.

NAOMI·DONALDSON

INTERMEDIATE ROOMS

THIRD, FOURTH, + FIFTH

Date-Nut Pinwheels

Betty Crocker's Picture Cook Book

½ cup shortening (part butter)
1 cup brown sugar, packed
1 egg
½ tsp. vanilla extract
1¾ cups flour
½ tsp. soda
¼ tsp. salt

Mix shortening, sugar, egg and vanilla thoroughly. Sift dry ingredients and stir in. Chill dough. Divide dough in half. Roll each piece of dough on waxed paper into rectangle about 7x11-inches. Spread rectangles with Date-Nut Filling (below). Roll up tightly, beginning at wide side. Pinch edge to seal. Wrap each roll in waxed paper and chill several hours. Heat oven to 400 degrees. Cut in ¼ inch slices. Place on greased baking sheet. Bake about 10 minutes or until lightly brown.

Date-Nut Filling: Cook in saucepan until slightly thickened, stirring constantly.
¾ pound pitted dates, cut-up **⅓ cup sugar** **⅓ cup water**
Remove from heat. Cool. Stir in **½ cup finely chopped nuts.**

German Pfeffernuesse (German Pepper Nut Cookies)

½ cup molasses
¼ cup honey
¼ cup butter, cubed
¼ cup shortening
2 eggs
2 tsp. anise extract
4 cups flour
¾ cup sugar
½ cup brown sugar
2 tsp. cinnamon
1½ tsp. baking soda
½ tsp. salt
1 tsp. ginger
1 tsp. cardamom (opt.)
1 tsp. nutmeg
1 tsp. cloves
1 tsp. pepper, coarse
1 cup powdered sugar

In a small saucepan, combine the molasses, honey, butter and shortening. Cook and stir over medium heat until melted. Remove from the heat; cool to room temperature. Stir in eggs and extract.

Combine the flour, sugar, brown sugar, cinnamon, baking soda, ginger, nutmeg, cloves, pepper and salt. Gradually add molasses mixture and mix well. Cover and refrigerate for at least 2 hours or overnight.

Roll dough into 1-inch balls. Place one inch apart on greased baking sheets. Bake at 325 degrees for 12-15 minutes or until golden brown. Remove cookies to wire racks. Roll warm cookies in powdered sugar. Cool completely. Store in an airtight container.

Date Cornflake Cookies

adapted from Great Grandma Mehmke's recipe

1¼ cups brown sugar
1 cup butter
2 eggs
2 tsp. vanilla extract
2 cups flour
1 tsp. baking powder
1 tsp. baking soda
1 cup coconut
½ cup chopped cherries
1 cup chopped dates
1 cup chopped walnuts
½ cup crushed cornflakes

Combine flour baking powder and soda. Cream butter and sugar; add eggs and vanilla and beat until light and fluffy. Gradually add sifted dry ingredients. Stir in coconut, nuts, dates, cherries and cornflakes. Mix as usual. Drop by spoonfuls onto ungreased cookie sheet. Flatten slightly with bottom of glass dipped in additional crushed cornflakes or sugar.

Bake at 350 degrees for 12 to 15 minutes. Drizzle with icing when cooled or place a piece of cherry on top of cookies before baking.

Icing: Melt **2 Tbsp. butter;** then add:
1 cup powdered sugar **1 Tbsp. hot water** **1 tsp. vanilla extract**

Mrs. Donaldson had no problem with hugging or touching students to encourage them. Discipline wasn't a real problem back then. If it was needed though, sitting out in the hallway was the method of choice. The hallway that connected the three classrooms and bathrooms wasn't that long. Everyone knew who was in trouble when they were found out there in the hall, and the word spread fast. I only had to sit in the hall once. I tried to hide behind the coats hanging on the hooks on the wall so as not to be detected. The hiding caused more of a hoot than if I had just taken my lumps like everyone else did.

Mrs. D. kept us all busy with reading and assignments when she was working with another class. There was no time for nonsense until recess time. We found lots of things to do then. Our favorite winter-time lunch and recess activity was to ice skate on the new ice rink across the highway in Hooper Park. That rink was built to replace the one we lost for the Texaco station.

Art was always fun since Mrs. D. had so many ideas and projects for us to work on. We were so fortunate and blessed to have had the artistic talents of June Petek and Mrs. Donaldson back then. Individually, they were each an artist on their own merits. When they worked together and combined their talents they came up with some very memorable and really neat ideas along with the cool parties and programs they put together.

June Petek's artistic talents inspired my sister to draw. She developed a passion for drawing and painting as a child. She loved horses and was constantly drawing and painting them. (My sister, Donna was the head bunny in the photos a few pages back in the Christmas program.)

Donna drew this picture of the Donaldson house from a photo, as she has done with several of the homes drawn in this book.

June hand-painted sweatshirts for many children with their names on them and a cartoon character of each child doing what they loved to do. Donna's shirt had a goofy looking girl playing a guitar. My sweatshirt had a character (like the one on page 13) making a mess in the kitchen. We all loved those sweatshirts. Donna has kept hers all these years. I wore mine out without realizing its sentimental value.

SCHOOL 1ST GRADE

(STARTING ON TOP ROW, LEFT TO RIGHT) CINDY LEIGLAND, BECKY YOUDERIAN, DONNA HAMMER, CATHIE PETEK, FRANCES WILLIAMS, SARAH MINNIS, VONNIE BARHAM, BUTCH GEHRING, MIKE HUBBARD, AND LAURA HOPKINS

Spritz *Betty Crocker's Cooky Book*

1 cup butter or margarine **⅔ cup sugar**
3 egg yolks **2½ cups flour, sifted**
1 tsp. each of almond and vanilla flavoring

Heat oven to 400 degrees. Mix butter, sugar, egg yolks, and flavoring thoroughly. Work in flour. Using ¼ of dough at a time, force dough through cookie press on ungreased baking sheet in desired shapes. Bake 7 to 10 minutes, until set but not brown.

Chocolate Spritz: Make spritz (above) except blend **2 squares (2 oz.) unsweetened chocolate (2 oz.)** melted into the shortening mixture.

Holiday Spritz: Make spritz (above) except omit almond or vanilla flavoring and add **1 tsp. rum** flavoring. Tint dough delicate pastel shades with food coloring. If desired, glaze cooled cookies with Butter Rum Glaze (below).

Butter Rum Glaze: Melt **¼ cup butter** in saucepan. Blend in **1 cup sifted powdered sugar** and **1 tsp. rum flavoring**. Stir in **1 to 2 Tbsp. hot water** until glaze is spreading consistency. Tint glaze to match cookies.

Viennese Shortbread

1 cup butter or margarine **2 cups flour**
½ cup sifted powdered sugar **½ tsp. vanilla**
¼ tsp. baking powder

Heat oven to 375 degrees. Cream butter, powdered sugar and vanilla until fluffy. Blend in sifted flour and baking powder; using medium bar design in cookie press. Press out strips, 3 inches long, on ungreased baking sheet, placing about an inch apart. (*If dough does not come through press smoothly, add 1 or 2 tsp. cream*). Bake about 7 minutes, or until very lightly browned around the edges. Cool. Put 2 cookies together with filling. For a fancier trim, the ends of cookies may be dipped in sweet chocolate.

Mocha Filling: Mix ⅔ cups sifted powdered sugar, 2 Tbsp. soft butter, and 1 tsp. powdered instant coffee dissolved in 1 tsp. boiling water until fluffy. If too dry, add a few drops of water.

How to make perfect Pressed Cookies:
Mix dough as directed. Dough for pressed cookies is high in shortening. Dough must be pliable. If very warm, chill a short time. (If too cold, it crumbles). Place dough in cookie press. Force dough through cookie press, on ungreased baking sheet. If baking sheet is to warm, fat in the dough will melt and cookies will pull away from sheet when press is lifted. Bake until set.

June Petek's name is nowhere to be found in "The Evergreen" as part of the annual staff. We all knew that she was the major contributor for this production, since artwork and printing were her specialty. We all discovered that her humility, encouragement and behind the scenes leadership were just a few more of her gifts. Many of her illustrations and advertisements have been used throughout this cookbook. Photos from the annual have also been used when telling about various families and their contributions to our community.

"The Evergreen" featured our teachers, annual staff, cheerleaders, basketball and volleyball teams, advertisers, teachers and each class.

The Lincoln Community Hall was not only used as the theater for movies, Christmas programs, dances and community benefits, but was also our gymnasium.

EILEEN SALMEN, CLAUDIA WILDIN, BEVERLY DIDRIKSEN

Cheer Leaders

VOLLEYBALL

(LEFT TO RIGHT, STARTING ON TOP ROW) DOUG D'AVIS, CONNIE HOPKINS, MIKE BEST PAUL GROSFIELD, MYRNA WELLS, PENNY MILLIRON, JANE LANTIS, PEGGY BEST, JOE YOUDERIAN, RICHARD OLSON, HARRY BRUNETT, BEV DIDRIKSEN, LYNN ELLIS, CLAUDIA WILDIN, DIANA WELCH, EILEEN SALMEN

Girl's Basketball

(TOP ROW, LEFT TO RIGH PENNY MILLIRON, SANDR BLUME, PEGGY-JO BEST, BEVERLY DIDRIKSEN, LYN ELLIS, EILEEN SALMEN, J LANTIS, PHYLLIS WELLS, CLAUDIA WILDIN, DIANA WELCH.

Frosted Molasses Cookies

1 cup butter (softened)
1 cup sugar
3 egg yolks
1 cup molasses
½ cup water
5 cups flour
3 tsp. baking soda
1½ tsp. ground cinnamon
1 tsp. baking powder

In a large bowl, cream butter and sugar until light and fluffy. Beat in the egg yolks, molasses and water. Combine the dry ingredients, sift and gradually add to creamed mixture and mix well. Cover and chill for 2 hours.
On a lightly floured surface, roll out dough to ⅛ inch thickness. Cut with a 2½ inch round cookie cutter. Place 1 inch apart on ungreased baking sheets. Bake at 375 degrees for 8 to 10 minutes, or until edges are firm. Remove to wire rack to cool.

Frosting: 1½ cup sugar
¼ cup water
3 egg whites
1 cup powdered sugar

Combine the sugar, egg whites and water in a small heavy saucepan (or double boiler) over low heat. With a hand mixer, beat on low speed for 1 minute. Continue beating over low heat until frosting reaches 160 degrees, about 8 to 10 minutes. Pour into a large bowl; add powdered sugar. Beat on high until frosting forms stiff peaks, about 7 minutes. Frost cookies. Let stand until dry.

Gingerbread Men

½ cup butter, softened
¾ cup packed brown sugar
⅓ cup molasses
2 Tbsp. water
2⅔ cups flour
1 tsp. baking soda
½ tsp. salt
2 tsp. ground ginger
½ tsp. each cinnamon, nutmeg and allspice

In a large bowl, cream butter and brown sugar until light and fluffy. Add the molasses, egg and water and beat well. Combine and sift the dry ingredients and add to creamed mixture and mix well. Divide the dough in half. Refrigerate for 30 minutes or until easy to handle. On a lightly floured surface, roll out each portion of dough to ⅛ inch thickness. Cut with a 4 inch cookie cutter. Place 2 inches apart on greased baking sheets. Re-roll scraps. Bake at 350 degrees for 8 to 10 minutes or until edges are firm. Remove to wire racks to cool completely. Decorate as desired.

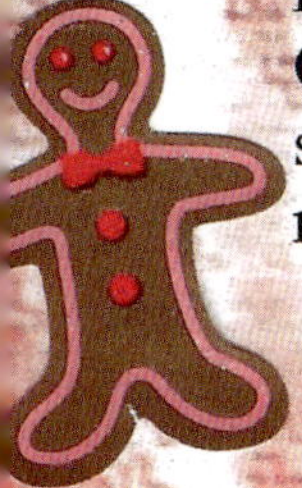

Ginger Creams

Betty Crocker's Cook Book

Mix thoroughly together: **¼ cup soft shortening, ½ cup sugar, 1 egg, ½ cup molasses**
Stir in: **1 tsp. soda dissolved in ½ cup hot water**
Sift together and stir in: **2 cups flour, ½ tsp. salt, 1 tsp. ginger, ½ tsp. each cinnamon, cloves and nutmeg**
Chill the dough. Drop rounded teaspoonful 2 inches apart on greased cookie sheet. Bake at 400 degrees for 7 to 8 minutes until set (no finger print remains when dented). While warm, frost with Quick Cream Icing.

Quick Cream Icing:
¾ cup powdered sugar, ¼ tsp. vanilla extract and cream (about 1 Tbsp.) to make easy to spread. Place a walnut half on center of cookie for decoration, if desired.

CLASSMATES

I do not remember who all the students are in this 1957 class photo, especially the smaller third graders in the front row. This is the 3rd, 4th and 5th grades.

In the back row, starting with the third person from the left are: Becky Youderian, Laura Hopkins, Sandy Maki, Donna Hammer, Karleen Hammer, Cathie Petek, Bob McClure and Lyle Clausen. Middle row (left to right) are: Donald Samatore, ?, Mary Grosfield, ?, Bob Lantis, Steve Welch, Jim Orr and Pat Evans. In the first row, I only know the first 2 boys, Alan Miliron and Butch Gehring and the first girl is Amy Miliron. Mrs. Donaldson was our teacher for those three grades.

2ND GRADE

I ♥ SCHOOL

(LEFT TO RIGHT, TOP) MARY GROSFIELD, BONNIE BLUME, KARLENE HAMMER, LYNN SHERLOCK, ANN BEST, BOBBY Mc CLURE, TERRY LEIGLAND, SANDRA MAKI, LINDA HUBBARD, JIMMY TILLOTSON, BOBBY LANTIS, KEITH DUSKY, STEVE WELCH

A+

(LEFT TO RIGHT, TOP ROW), MARILYN PHELDT, CONNIE PETEK, LYNN ELLIS, DIANA WELCH, DONALD SAMITORE, DANNY LANTIS, BILL MINNIS, PHYLLIS WELLS, CLAUDIA WILDIN

3RD Ala GRADE

MY FRIENDS

Cream Wafers *Betty Crocker's Cooky Book*

1 cup butter or margarine **2 cups flour**
⅓ cup whipping cream (35%) butterfat granulated sugar
Creamy Butter Filling (below)

Mix butter, cream and sifted flour thoroughly. Chill 1 hour. Heat oven to 375 degrees. Roll dough ⅛ inch thick on lightly floured board. Cut into 1½ inch rounds. Transfer to waxed paper heavily sprinkled with sugar, turning to coat both sides. Place on ungreased baking sheet. Prick in 4 places with fork. Bake 7 to 9 minutes or until slightly puffy. Put two cooled cookies together with Filling.

Creamy Butter Filling: Blend **¼ cup soft butter, ¾ cup sifted powdered sugar, 1 egg yolk and 1 tsp. vanilla**. If desired, tint pink or green.

Thumbprint Cookies

½ cup shortening (part butter or margarine)
¼ cup brown sugar, packed
1 egg, separated
½ tsp. vanilla
1 cup flour
¼ tsp. salt
¾ cup finely chopped nuts
jelly or tinted butter cream icing

Heat oven to 350 degrees. Mix shortening, sugar, egg yolk and vanilla thoroughly. Sift flour and salt together and stir in. Roll dough into (1 tsp.) ball. Beat egg white slightly with fork. Dip balls in egg white. Roll in nuts. Place about 1 inch apart on ungreased baking sheet; press thumb gently in center of each. Bake 10 to 12 minutes or until set. Cool. Fill thumbprints with jelly or tinted Creamy Butter Filling (above).

Gumdrop Cookies

1 cup shortening
1 cup brown sugar
1 cup sugar
1 tsp. vanilla
2 eggs
2 cups flour
1 tsp. baking powder
½ tsp. salt
½ tsp. soda
1 cup coconut
2 cups oatmeal
1 cup gumdrops, cut up

Cream shortening and sugars. Add eggs and beat well. Add vanilla. Sift dry ingredients and add, then add oats, coconut and gumdrops Roll into small balls; place on a greased cookie sheet, press flat with a fork. Bake at 375 degrees for 10 minutes.

Sugared Cherry Jewels

1 cup butter, softened
½ cup sugar
⅓ cup light corn syrup
2 egg yolks
½ tsp. vanilla
2½ cups flour
1 jar (10 oz.) maraschino cherries, drained and halved
Additional sugar

Cream butter and sugar. Beat in corn syrup, egg yolks and vanilla. Gradually add flour and mix well. Cover and refrigerate for 1 hour or until easy to handle. Roll into 1-inch balls; roll each ball in additional sugar. Place 2 inches apart on baking sheets. Make an indentation in the center of each. Press a cherry half in the center. Bake at 325 degrees for 15 minutes.

PAT · SHERLOCK
PRIMARY ROOMS
FIRST AND SECOND

Annual Staff

Faculty

CLASS OFFICERS

1955

EDITOR
MIKE BEST

BUSINESS · MANAGER
PAUL GROSFIELD

ASST. · EDITOR
SHARON WIEDERHOLD

ANNUAL STAFF · left to right · MIKE BEST, PAUL GROSFIELD, DOUG D'AVIS, SHARON WIEDERHOLD, MITZI GRANTIER, CONNIE HOPKINS, DOLORES BROWN, PENNY MILLIRON.

SPONSOR · ·
HENRY SHERLOCK

PRESIDENT · ·
MICHAEL BEST
VICE-PRESIDENT · ·
PAUL GROSFIELD
SECRETARY · ·
DOUGLAS D'AVIS
TREASURER · ·
MYRNA WELLS

HENRY · SHERLOCK
UPPER ROOMS
SIXTH, SEVENTH, + EIGHTH

Best Teacher EVER!

Almond Roca Bars

1 cup butter
½ cup brown sugar
2 cups flour
½ cup white sugar
1 tsp. vanilla
1 egg
¼ tsp. salt

Mix all ingredients by hand. Place on cookie sheet and flatten out ¼ to ½ inch thick. Bake at 350 degrees for 15 to 20 minutes. While warm, spread with a **9 oz. Hershey bar** and top with **ground nuts**. Cut and refrigerate.

Frosted Chocolate Drops

1 cup shortening
2 cups brown sugar, packed
2 eggs
2 tsp. vanilla
1 cup milk or buttermilk
3⅓ cups sifted flour
¼ cup cocoa
1 tsp. baking soda
1 tsp. salt
Mocha Frosting (recipe follows)

Cream together shortening and brown sugar until light and fluffy. Add eggs, one at a time, beating well after each addition. Blend in vanilla. Sift together all dry ingredients. Add dry ingredients alternating with milk to creamed mixture, beating well after each addition. Drop by teaspoonful's about 2 inches apart on greased baking sheets.

Bake in 350 degree oven for 10 minutes or until done. Remove from baking sheets; cool on racks. Frost with **Mocha Frosting**: Combine **¼ cup cocoa, ½ cup soft butter or margarine, 1 tsp. vanilla and 3 cups sifted powdered sugar**. Gradually stir in **¼ cup hot coffee**. Beat until smooth and of spreading consistency.

Frosted Peanut Cookies

1 cup butter, softened
1½ cups brown sugar, packed
2 eggs
1 tsp. vanilla
2 cups flour
2 tsp. baking powder
1 cup salted peanuts, chopped
1 cup oatmeal

In a large bowl, cream butter and brown sugar until light and fluffy. Beat in eggs and vanilla. Combine flour and baking powder; gradually add to creamed mixture and mix well. Stir in oats and peanuts. Drop by rounded teaspoonfuls 2 inches apart onto baking sheets. Bake at 350 degrees for 10 to 12 minutes.

Frosting: Beat following ingredients until smooth then frost cookies.

½ cup peanut butter
3 cups confectioners' sugar
⅓ cup milk

Chocolate Crinkles

½ cup vegetable oil
4 sq. (4 oz.) unsweetened chocolate melted
4 eggs (blend in one at a time)
2 cups sugar
2 tsp. vanilla
2 cups flour
2 tsp. baking powder
½ tsp. salt

Cream oil, chocolate, sugar, eggs and vanilla together. Blend in sifted dry ingredients. Chill several hours. Drop teaspoonful's of dough into powdered sugar (1 cup). Roll in sugar and shape into balls. Bake at 350 degrees for 10 to 12 minutes on greased baking sheet.

Meanwhile back at the schoolhouse, things were never quite the same after Mr. Donaldson died. Mrs. Donaldson's outgoing personality was subdued by loneliness and grief as would be expected. She was still a great teacher but retired from teaching in the spring of 1957. She left Lincoln after she retired, but didn't leave for good. She returned some years later after she had remarried, with her new husband. Hank Underwood was a chef, and together they ran Lambkin's Restaurant for several years. He was the cook and she was the hostess. So with her beautiful dresses, high heels and jewelry to match, stylish haircuts, perfect posture, pose and vibrant personality, she was the "hostess with the mostess" and made dining at Lambkin's an uptown type of experience.

I will always appreciate having had Mrs. Donaldson as a teacher and a ladylike role model. She instilled a thirst for knowledge, reading, education, adventure and fun in her students. We were so blessed that she was there for us during such a critical part of our lives.

Proverbs 15:2 "A wise teacher makes learning a joy."

4TH GRADE

(LEFT TO RIGHT, TOP ROW), IRVIN WIEDERHOLD, EDDY PERKL, SANDRA BLUME, JANE LANTIS, EILEEN SALMEN, AND NORMAN GROSFIELD

FIFTH·GRADE

(LEFT TO RIGHT) SAMMY DEAN, PEGGY BEST, BEVERLY DIDRIKSEN, AND TOMMY BRUNETT

In Memory

Phyllis Wells
Beverly

"Cousins"
Lynn Ellis
Terry Routzahn

Frozen Fruit Cookies Betty Crocker's Cooky Book

1 cup butter or margarine
1 cup sifted powdered sugar
1 egg
2½ cups flour
¼ tsp. cream of tartar
½ cup pecans, chopped
1 cup whole candied fruit, such as cherries (red &/or green)
½ cup chopped candied fruit or citron

Cream butter and sugar, beat in the egg. Stir in flour and cream of tartar. Blend in pecans and fruit. Form in rolls 1½" in diameter. Wrap in foil or transparent plastic wrap, freeze. Heat oven to 375 degrees. Slice very thinly. Place on greased baking sheet. Bake 6 to 8 minutes.

Melt-a-way Cookies Nellie Knight

1 cup powdered sugar
1 cup white sugar
1 cup oil
1 cup butter
2 eggs
2 tsp. vanilla extract
1 tsp. almond extract, optional
4 cups + 4 Tbsp. of flour
1 tsp. salt
1 tsp. cream of tartar
1 tsp. baking soda

Cream sugars, butter, oil and eggs. Sift dry ingredients together and add to the creamed mixture. Add vanilla. Cool cookie dough in refrigerator. Make balls and flatten with a glass dipped in sugar or colored sprinkles. Bake at 350 degrees for 15 minutes.

Peanut Butter Cups Peggy Knight
Lincoln School Cookbook

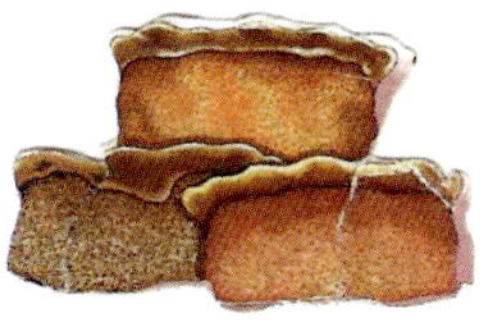

1¾ stick margarine
1 cup peanut butter
2½ cups powdered sugar
1 package graham crackers, crushed
1 cup milk chocolate chips

Melt margarine and peanut butter. Stir in sugar and cracker crumbs. Pat into a 9 x 13-inch cake pan. Cover with chocolate chips. Sit in warm oven until chips are soft enough to spread. Cut into squares and cool in refrigerator.

Candy Cane Cookies Betty Crocker's Cooky Book

1 cup shortening (½ butter or margarine)
1 cup sifted powdered sugar
1 egg
1½ tsp. almond extract
½ cup crushed peppermint candies
2½ cups flour
1 tsp. salt
½ tsp. red food coloring
1 tsp. vanilla
½ cup granulated sugar

Heat oven to 375 degrees. Mix shortening, sugar, egg and flavorings thoroughly. Sift flour and salt; stir into shortening mixture. Divide dough in half. Blend food coloring into one half. Roll a 4-inch strip (using 1 tsp. dough) from each color. For smooth, even strips, roll them back and forth on lightly floured board. Place strips side-by-side, press lightly together and twist like rope (see sketch). Roll lightly in mixture of candy and sugar after twisting them together. For best results, complete cookies one at a time. If all the dough of one color is shaped first, strips become too dry to twist. Place on greased baking sheet. Curve top down to form handle of cane. Bake about 9 minutes, until lightly browned. While still warm, remove from baking sheet with spatula sprinkle with rest of candy and sugar mixture.

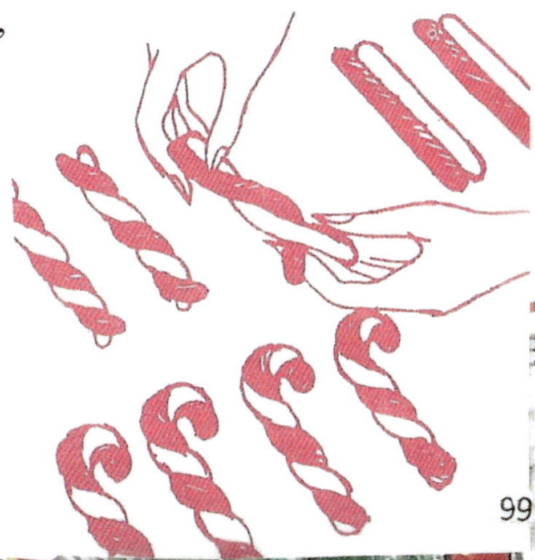

Sixth Grade

{LEFT TO RIGHT} RICHARD OLSEN, DALE SALMEN, PENNY MILLIRON, DAVID SAMITORE, TIM D'AVIS, AND HARRY BRUNETT.

6TH GRADE

Seventh Grade

WHO'S WHO

7TH GRADE

{LEFT · TO · RIGHT} CONNIE HOPKINS, JOE MINNIS, JOE YOUDERIAN, MYRNA WELLS

8TH GRADE

CLASS OF

Sharon Wiederhold, Mitzi Grantier, Dolores Brown, Mike Best, Paul Grosfield Frank Johnson, David Brown, Doug D'avis

After School Favorite Cookies

Chocolate Chip Cookies

⅔ cup shortening
⅔ cup butter or margarine
1 cup sugar
1 cup brown sugar
2 eggs
2 tsp. vanilla extract
3 cups flour
1 tsp. salt
1 tsp. soda
1 cup chopped nuts
1 to 2 pkgs. (12 oz.) chocolate chips

Cream shortening, butter, sugars, eggs and vanilla. Sift dry ingredients and stir into shortening mixture. Stir in nuts and chocolate chops. Bake 8 to 10 minutes at 350 degrees.

Peanut Butter Cookies

1 cup shortening
1 cup peanut butter
1 cup granulated sugar
1 cup brown sugar
2 eggs
2½ cups flour
1 tsp. baking powder
1½ tsp. soda
½ tsp. salt

Mix shortening, peanut butter, sugars and egg thoroughly. Sift and blend all dry ingredients and stir into shortening mixture.
Heat oven to 375 degrees. Roll dough in ¼-inch balls. Place 3 inches apart on lightly greased baking sheet. Flatten crisscross style with fork dipped in flour. Bake 10 to 12 minutes.

Gingersnaps

Dorothy Anderson

¾ cup shortening
1 cup sugar
¼ cup molasses
1 egg
2 cups flour
¼ tsp. salt
2 tsp. soda
1 tsp. each cinnamon, cloves and ginger

Cream shortening and sugar. Add egg and molasses and beat well. Sift dry ingredients together and add to shortening mixture. Mix well. Roll into small balls; then roll in sugar. Place on a greased cookie sheet 2½ inches apart. Bake at 375 degrees for 10 minutes.

Rice Krispies Bars

½ cup butter
1 (16 oz.) pkg. marshmallows
7 to 8 cups rice krispies

Melt butter in a 3-qt. saucepan over low heat. Add marshmallows, stir until melted and well blended. Remove from heat. Stir in cereal until well coated. Press into a 9 x 13-inch pan.

The Community Hall

Drawing by June Petek

The Lincoln Community Hall was, and still is, the center for most activities in the area. I often wonder if having the Community Hall in the middle of Lincoln isn't the glue that holds the community together. It is a place where most of the community can gather together for a function, socialize for a few hours and leave with a feeling of belonging in a community with a lot of caring and wonderful people.

The history of the hall is a great story in chapter 9 of the Lincoln history book *Gold Pans and Singletrees* which states that "the Community Hall is central to many of the memories of the Upper Blackfoot Valley (p. 123). The article also features the writing of C.V. Rubottom about the construction of the hall in his unpublished "Montana Memories." In his writing, he told how meetings were held and an association was formed that drew up the plans for the octagonal log building with a maple dance floor.

Tom Hensler, an early pioneer and carpenter in the Lincoln Valley, was hired as the supervisor for the building project. The building was completed in two years with donated labor. The logs were cut in the woods on Stonewall Creek about five miles from the site of the hall.

Lincoln Community Hall by Nina Baril

Photo from "Story of Lincoln"–A Montana Centennial Project by the Pinegrove Extension Homemakers, 1989

"We finished the hall in February of 1918 and held our dedication dance on the night of the 22nd" (1994, p. 124). Dances were held almost weekly during the summer months after the close of WWI as everyone was crazy about dancing. Crowds soon came from Helena and Great Falls to attend the summer dances. Local talent was available to furnish the music at first, and then outside music was hired as the people wanted more sophisticated talent. The local people made enough money the first summer from their dances to build a large addition on the back side of the hall for a dining room. "This completed the finest hall in central Montana, and several places copied our plan" (1994, p. 125). After completion of the main hall, Len Lambkin donated the land to help with the addition of a kitchen and a dining/meeting area to the log structure. The back wall of the new dining room was lined with bookshelves. This was the start of Lincoln's first library with Mary Lambkin donating many of the books.

The Lincoln Community Hall has been used as a school and a church, for weddings, funerals. classes, receptions, plays, meetings, banquets, concerts, community fund-raisers, bazaars and craft shows, as a gym for basketball games and practice sessions (before the new school and gym were built), as a library and movie theater, and for the annual Hunter's Stew Dinner, the Fireman's Ball and many other community benefits and functions.

I remember June Petek teaching first-aid classes to our Girl Scout troop in the dining room, and how warm and cozy it was with a stove near the outside door. Of course, June brightened up the room with her presence, no matter how cold it was outside. As a child, the dining room seemed so large and the kitchen was small. There has been some remodeling done somewhere along the line, as the kitchen area is now much larger and the dining area is just large enough to fit four tables, with just enough room behind the tables for the servers to do their work. All dining now takes place in the main part of the hall.

Some of my favorite memories of the Community Hall were the dances with basket socials and auctions that even the children could attend with their parents. The lunch baskets were auctioned off to the highest bidder, who then got to eat lunch with the lady who furnished the basket.

Cakes and other food item goodies were also auctioned off. Some of the big sellers were Olga Perkle's dill pickles, Bernice Lambkin's German chocolate cake and Signe Grosfield's homemade breads. I even used to bake and decorate Christmas tree cutout cookies to be auctioned off.

My favorite memories though, are of the Christmas program. The program was the biggest event of the year and always included the real Christmas story, the birth of baby Jesus. Bob McClure and I were the tallest in our class, so we usually played Joseph and Mary, with my doll as baby Jesus. There was also a sing-along with the audience of the old Christmas carols. Everyone knew the tune and words by heart. After the program, the visit by Santa Claus added to the excitement of the evening. The Lambkin sister, Ellen Mulcare, Virginia Horner and Betty Disney told their version of their memories of Santa's arrival at the Community Halls in *Gold Pans and Sjngletrees.*

The community Christmas tree and school program held at the hall was the highlight of the winter—especially for the children. The men would see to it that one of the most perfect trees in the forest was brought in to be decorated—right to the top, touching the ceiling of the hall. The teacher worked long and hard getting the school children ready for the program that always pleased the audience, especially the parent, and each and every child participated, dressed in their finest and faces shining. The end of the program always signaled the arrival of Santa. We'd hear his sleigh bells in the distance and a hush would fall over the place. Then the words 'Whoa Prancer! Whoa Dancer!' and parents had to hold their children to keep them from storming the door. And in would come that magical man, 'Ho, Ho, Ho—Merry Christmas everyone.' And he was besieged by the braver ones—some hanging back a little. It never occurred to me that it might be Bob Fisk or maybe, Ed Grantier, in a Santa suit and if there were those that doubted---they never let it be known—not then. Each child received a wrapped gift from the community plus a bag of Christmas candy and an apple and orange (1994, p. 85).

By the time I was in school, getting a gift for each child was too much, due to the larger size of our classes. We did get the bag of candy though, and with an apple and an orange, we thought that was the greatest.

When I had children of my own, I would always put an apple and an orange in their Christmas stockings along with candy and a small gift. One time they asked "What's the deal with the apple and orange? We have a refrigerator full of them." I then realized that back in those days, fresh fruit in the winter was a "big deal" and a real luxury.

Cranberry Chiffon Pie

1 (9-inch) baked pie crust
⅛ tsp. salt
¾ cup sugar
3 egg whites
1 tsp. vanilla
1 Tbsp. unflavored gelatin
2½ cup fresh cranberries
2 tsp. grated orange rind
6 Tbsp. sugar
½ cup whipping cream
¼ cup water
½ cup cold water
¼ cup orange juice

Soften gelatin in ¼ cup water. In a saucepan cook cranberries in ½ cup water or less, add ¾ cup sugar and salt. Cook until berries pop open. Stir occasionally. Blend in orange rind, orange juice and gelatin. Chill to thicken. (This mixture may be made the night before.) Next day whip egg whites until stiff peaks form, and then gradually add sugar and vanilla. Fold the whipped cream and then fold the egg whites into cranberry mixture. Pour entire mixture into baked pie shell. Chill until ready to serve.

Sour Cream Apple/Craisin Pie

2 Tbsp. flour
¼ tsp. nutmeg
1 tsp. vanilla extract
1 unbaked (9-inch) pie shell
¼ tsp. salt
1 cup dairy sour cream
2 cups diced peeled apples
¾ cup sugar
1 egg
1 cup Craisins or raisins

Topping:

⅓ cup sugar
1 tsp. cinnamon
⅓ cup flour
2 Tbsp. butter

Sift together flour, salt, sugar and nutmeg into bowl. Combine egg, sour cream and vanilla. Add to dry ingredients; mix well. Stir in apples and Craisins. Spoon into pie shell. Bake in 400 degree oven 15 minutes. Reduce heat to 350 degrees and continue baking 30 min. Combine topping ingredients. Mix until crumbly. Remove pie from oven. Increase oven to 400 degrees. Sprinkle topping over filling. Return pie to oven and bake 10 minutes more. Cool

Cranberry Raspberry Pie

2 cups cranberries, fresh or frozen and thawed
1 (10 oz.) pkg. frozen red raspberries, thawed
2 Tbsp. quick cooking tapioca
1 Tbsp. butter or margarine
1½ cups sugar
½ tsp. salt
¼ tsp. almond extract
Almond Pastry (below)

Chop or coarsely grind cranberries. Combine with raspberries, sugar, salt, tapioca and almond extract; mix well. Spoon into pastry-lined pie plate. Dot with butter. Roll out remaining dough, cut in ½-inch strips. Interlace strips in crisscross fashion over filling to make lattice top. Trim strips even with pie edge. Turn bottom crust up over end of strips. Press firmly to seal edge. Flute edge. Bake in 425 degree oven 10 minutes. Reduce heat to 350 degrees and bake 40 minutes or until golden brown and filling is bubbly. Cool on rack.

Almond Pastry: Sift together: **2¼ cups sifted flour, 1 tsp. salt and 1 Tbsp. sugar.** Cut in: **¾ cup shortening** until mixture resembles fine crumbs. Beat together in a cup: **1 egg yolk, 2 tsp. almond extract and ¼ cup water**; sprinkle over flour mixture. Toss with fork to make soft dough. Divide dough in half; form each half into a ball. Flatten half of dough on lightly floured surface. Roll to about ⅛ inch thickness and line 9-inch pie plate.

Bridger and Dawson Moyer

I don't think the Christmas programs are as big of a deal now as they were back then either. Since my kids are grown and gone, it is the church programs that attract us and our kids now. There is usually a Christmas Eve service, then dinner, Christmas Eve presents and games.

On Christmas morning, there is a big breakfast before traveling to Great Falls to spend the day with our parents, who aren't able to travel anymore. Andrew, our oldest grandson, who is now about grown, is the pancake specialist of the family. Christmas morning is his time to shine in the kitchen with his whole-wheat pancake recipe.

A visit to see Santa is still a big deal even if it doesn't look like it on the faces of my youngest grandsons, Bridger and Dawson Moyer.

Santa seems to shows up in more places before the holidays these days. He has increased the size of his territory far beyond the walls of the Lincoln Community Hall.

The Moyer boys 2014

Bridger, Rhett and Dawson Moyer

The Hammel Family

The Hammel Grandkids

Sydney
Cody
Seth
Lane

Merry Christmas

AND HAPPY NEW YEAR

Santa Pancakes

Jace Butcher

2 cups biscuit/baking mix
1 tsp. ground cinnamon
2 egg, beaten
1 cup milk
1 tsp. vanilla extract
2 medium bananas, sliced
18 semisweet chocolate chips
1 can (21 oz.) cherry pie filling
Whipped cream in a can

In a large bowl, combine baking mix and cinnamon. Combine the egg, milk and vanilla; stir into dry ingredients just until moistened. Pour batter by ¼ cupfuls onto a greased hot griddle. Turn when bubbles form on top; cook until second side is golden brown. Place pancakes on individual plates. For Santa's eyes, place two banana slices on each pancake. Top each with a chocolate chip. For ears, cut remaining banana slices in half; place on either side of pancake. For nose, remove nine cherries from pie filling; place one in the center of each pancake. Spoon ¼ cup pie filling above pancake for hat. Use whipped cream to spray the beard, hat brim and pom-pom.

Whole Wheat Pancakes

Andrew Butcher

1 cup flour
1 cup whole wheat flour
4 tsp. baking powder
¼ cup sugar
2 eggs
2 cups milk
¼ cup oil

Mix dry ingredients together. Mix wet ingredients together. Combine both and mix well enough to get all the lumps out. Pour batter by ¼ cupfuls onto a greased hot griddle. Turn when bubbles form on top. Cook until brown.

Cranberry Nut Bread

McKensie Butcher

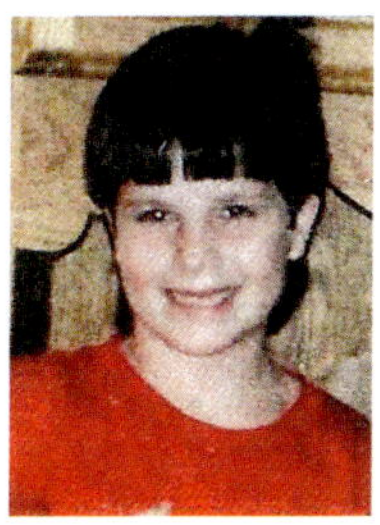

2 eggs
1 cup sugar
⅓ cup margarine, melted
1¼ cup fresh or frozen whole cranberries
1 cup flour
1 tsp. baking powder
1 tsp. soda
1½ cup walnuts, chopped

Beat eggs until thick; gradually add sugar, beating until blended. Stir in sifted dry ingredients and melted butter. Add cranberries and nuts; stir until combined. Spread in a greased loaf pan and bake at 350 degrees for 1 hour.

Cranberry Dessert

Taylor Butcher

1 can whole berry cranberry sauce
1 tsp. grated orange peel
¼ tsp. ground allspice
1 cup heavy whipping cream, or 2 cups cool whip

In a large bowl, combine the cranberry sauce, orange peel and allspice. Fold in whipped cream. Spoon into dessert dished. Refrigerate until ready to serve. Top with grated orange peel on top of spoonful of cream.

Raised Waffles with Strawberry-Rhubarb Compote

Adapted from Williams-Sonoma *Essentials of Breakfast and Brunch*

4 cups rhubarb stalks, coarsely chopped
¼ to ½ cup sugar (more to taste)
1½ cup strawberries, hulled and halved
¼ cup water

To make the compote, combine the rhubarb, sugar and water in a non-reactive saucepan over medium heat. Cook until the mixture begins to simmer and release liquid, about 10 minutes. Uncover and stir in the strawberries. Cook at a gentle simmer until the rhubarb is soft when pierced with a fork, about 10 minutes. Skim off any foam from the top and discard. Serve warm, or store in an airtight container in the refrigerator for up to 2 days. Warm over low heat before serving.

Raised Waffles:

1 pkg. (2½ tsp.) active dry yeast
1 tsp. granulated sugar
¼ cup warm water (105 to 115 degrees)
1 cup milk
2 Tbsp. unsalted butter
1 cup flour
2 tbsp. brown sugar, packed
¼ tsp. salt
Canola or corn oil, as needed for cooking
1 egg
1 tsp. baking soda

In a large bowl, dissolve the yeast and granulated sugar in the warm water and let stand until foamy, about 5 minutes. In a saucepan over low heat, combine the milk and butter and heat to lukewarm (about 115 degrees).

In a small bowl, whisk together the flour, brown sugar and salt. Stir the warm milk mixture into the dissolved yeast. Add the flour mixture and stir until blended. Cover the bowl and refrigerate overnight. The batter will thicken slightly.

Preheat a regular waffle maker for 5 minutes, and then lightly brush with oil. Stir the baking soda and egg into the chilled batter until blended. Ladle enough batter for 1 waffle into the center of the waffle maker (about ½ cup) and spread with a small spatula to fill the holes. Close the waffle maker and cook until the steam stops escaping from the sides and the lid opens easily, about 5 minutes. The waffle should be browned and crisp.

Strawberry Waffles

2½ cups flour **¾ tsp. salt**
4 tsp. baking powder
1½ Tbsp. white sugar
2 cups buttermilk **2 eggs**
½ cup vanilla yogurt (Greek style)
½ cup butter, melted
¾ cup chopped strawberries

Preheat and grease waffle iron. Sift dry ingredients together in a bowl. Whisk wet ingredients together in a separate bowl; stir into flour mixture until batter is smooth. Fold berries into batter. Pour about ⅓ cup batter into preheated waffle iron; cook until lightly browned, 5 to 7 minutes. Repeat with remaining batter.

ANYONE CARE FOR AN OLD FASHIONED WINTER PANCAKE SUPPER FUNDRAISER AT THE LINCOLN COMMUNITY HALL?

Photo courtesy of Roger Dey, BVD, 2015

Eggnog French Toast

3 to 4 eggs
big splash of eggnog
Pinch salt
Smidge of vanilla extract or rum flavoring

Mix up all of the above ingredients. Take **6 slices of bread** from the breadbox. Melt a blob of butter on pancake griddle for frying. While the pan is heating, dip bread in mixture and let it soak for a few seconds then fry it up until golden on both sides flipping half way through the cooking time. Top French toast with a skoosh of butter and slosh on your favorite syrup.

Strawberry Cheesecake French Toast

1 carton (8 oz.) ricotta cheese
3 Tbsp. powdered sugar
1 tsp. vanilla extract
16 slices French bread (½ inch thick)
1 cup milk **2 eggs**
2 cups sliced fresh or frozen strawberries
Additional powdered sugar or maple syrup for topping

In a small bowl, combine ricotta, sugar and vanilla; mix well. Spread 2 tablespoons mixture on eight slices of bread; cover with remaining bread. In a bowl, beat eggs and milk; soak sandwiches 1 to 2 minutes per side. Cook on a hot greased griddle for 5 minutes on each side or until golden brown and heated through. Serve with strawberries. Serve with sausage links.

Gingerbread Pancakes

1 cup flour **1 Tbsp. sugar** **½ tsp. salt**
1 tsp. baking powder **½ tsp. baking soda** **1 tsp. ginger**
Pinch ground cloves **½ tsp. ground cinnamon**

Combine all the above in a bowl. Combine the ingredients below and add to the dry ingredients.

1 cup buttermilk **2 Tbsp. molasses** **1 egg**
1 Tbsp. vegetable oil **maple syrup and whipped cream, optional**

Mix well. Pour batter by ¼ cupfuls onto a lightly greased hot griddle; turn when bubbles form on top of pancakes. Cook until second side is golden brown.

Candy Cane Cheesecake

Crust: **⅓ cup butter, melted**
1½ cups chocolate wafer crumbs **2 Tbsp. sugar**

Filling:
3 pkg. (8 oz. each) cream cheese, softened
¾ cup sugar
4 eggs
3 Tbsp. flour
¾ tsp. peppermint extract
1 cup sour cream
2 Tbsp. vanilla or white chips
Red food coloring
Crushed peppermint candy and whipped cream

Combine first three ingredients; press onto bottom of a greased 9-inch springform pan. Chill.
In a mixing bowl, beat cream cheese and sugar until smooth. Add flour; mix well. Add eggs, one at a time, beating just until blended. Stir in sour cream. Set aside.
In a small saucepan over low heat, melt vanilla chips. Remove from the heat. Add ¼ cup cream cheese mixture, extract and a few drops of food coloring; mix well. Pour half of the remaining cream cheese mixture over crust. Top with half of the peppermint mixture; swirl with a knife. Repeat layers.
Bake at 450 degrees for 10 minutes. Reduce heat to 250 degrees; bake 40 to 50 minutes longer or until the center is almost set. Cool on a wire rack for 1 hour. Chill at least 3 hours. Just before serving, remove sides of pan. Garnish with crushed candy and whipped topping.

Eggnog Cream Pies

2 unbaked pastry shells (9 inches)
4 oz. cream cheese, softened
½ cup powdered sugar
1 tsp. ground allspice and nutmeg
1 tsp. ground nutmeg
2 cartons one (8 oz.) and one (12 oz.) frozen whipped topping, thawed, divided
3 pkgs. (3.4 oz. each) instant cheesecake or vanilla pudding mix
3¾ cup cups cold eggnog
Additional ground nutmeg

Line unpricked pastry shells with a double thickness of heavy-duty foil. Bake at 450 degrees for 8 minutes. Remove foil; bake 5 minutes longer. Cool on wire racks.
In a small mixing bowl, beat the cream cheese, powdered sugar, allspice and nutmeg until smooth. Fold in the 8 oz. carton of whipped topping. Spoon into the crusts.
In a large bowl, whisk the eggnog and pudding mixes for 2 minutes. Let stand for 2 minutes or until soft-set. Spread over the cream cheese layer. Top the pies with remaining whipped topping; sprinkle with additional nutmeg. Cover and refrigerate for 8 hours or overnight.

Cranberry Ice Cream Pie

Pastry for single crust pie (9 inches)
1¼ cup jellied cranberry sauce
2 cups vanilla ice cream, softened
¼ cup orange juice concentrate, thawed
1 pkg. (3.4 oz.) instant vanilla pudding mix
½ cup heavy cream
Ground nutmeg

Line a 9-inch pie plate with pastry, trim and flute edges. Line unpricked pastry with a double thickness of heavy-duty foil. Bake at 450 degrees for 8 minutes. Remove foil; bake 5 to 7 minutes longer or until lightly browned. Spread cranberry sauce over bottom of pie crust; set aside. In a large bowl, combine the ice cream, juice concentrate and pudding mix. In a small bowl beat cream until soft peaks form; fold into ice cream mixture. Pour over cranberry sauce; sprinkle with nutmeg. Freeze until firm.

Fruity Cranberry Punch

4 cups cranberry juice, chilled
4 cups pineapple juice, chilled
2 cups sugar, divided
1 to 2 tsp. almond extract
½ gallon strawberry ice cream, softened
2 cups heavy whipping cream
1 liter ginger ale, chilled

In a large punch bowl, combine juices, 1½ cups sugar, almond extract and ice cream. Refrigerate until serving. Just before serving, beat cream in a mixing bowl. Gradually add the remaining sugar, beating until soft peaks form. Whisk gently into chilled juice mixture. Add ginger ale.

Cranberry Tea

1 bottle (32 oz.) cranberry juice
2 cups sugar
1 can (6 oz.) frozen orange juice concentrate
1 can (6 oz.) frozen lemonade concentrate
⅓ cup red hot candies
2 whole cloves

In a 3-qt. saucepan, combine all ingredients; bring to a boil over medium heat. Boil for 7 min. stirring occasionally. Remove cloves.
To serve, mix 1 cup concentrate and 2 cups water; heat through. Store concentrate in a covered container in the refrigerator. Yield: 18 cups.

Creamy Strawberry Breeze

2 cups whole strawberries
2 cups apple juice
3 cups whipping cream

Place half of the strawberries and apple juice in a blender; cover and process until smooth. Add half of the whipped topping; cover and process until blended. Pour into glasses.

Citrus Sunshine Punch

1 can (12 oz.) frozen lemonade concentrate, thawed
1 can (12 oz.) frozen limeade concentrate, thawed
1 can (12 oz.) frozen orange juice concentrate, thawed
2 quarts cold water
1 bottle (2 liters) ginger ale, chilled
Ice cubes and 1 quart orange sherbet

In a large container, combine concentrates with water; mix well. Chill. Just before serving, add ginger ale and ice cubes. Top with scoops of sherbet.

Orange Blush

1 can (12 oz.) frozen orange juice concentrate, thawed
2 cups cranberry juice
½ cup sugar
1 liter club soda, chilled
Crushed ice

In a large pitcher or bowl. Combine the orange juice concentrate, cranberry juice and sugar. Refrigerate for at least 1 hour; Just before serving, stir in soda. Serve over ice.

Orange Cranberry Tea Cookies

1 cup salted butter
½ cup sugar
1 tsp. vanilla
¾ cup dried cranberries, chopped
zest of 2 oranges, chopped fine
2 Tbsp. milk or cream
½ tsp. salt
2½ cups flour
½ cup pecans, chopped
¼ cup extra sugar

Cream butter and sugar until fluffy. Add milk and vanilla and mix. Add flour and salt and mix well. It might seem crumbly at this point but if you keep blending it will come together eventually. Add the cranberries, orange zest and pecans.

Roll into 2 logs about 8 x 1½ inches. Wrap and chill for 2 hours in the fridge. They can also be put in the freezer for 30 to 60 minutes. Slice rolls into ¼ inch thick cookies. Roll the edges of the cookie in sugar. Place on lightly greased cookie sheets. Bake at 375 degrees for 10 to 15 minutes. Don't over bake.

Orange Cranberry Muffins

2 cups flour
1 cup sugar
1½ tsp. baking powder
1 tsp. salt
½ tsp. baking soda
¼ cup shortening
1 egg, beaten
¾ cup orange juice
1 Tbsp. grated orange rind
1 cup coarsely chopped cranberries
¼ chopped walnuts
1 Tbsp. flour

Sift together 2 cups flour, sugar, baking powder, soda and salt. Cut in shortening until mixture resembles coarse meal. Combine egg, orange juice and orange rind in small bowl. Add to dry ingredients all at once; stir just until moistened. Combine cranberries, walnuts and 1 Tbsp. flour; stir into batter. Pour batter into greased 3-inch muffin pan cups, filling ⅔ full. Bake in a 400 degree oven for 20 minutes or until done. Makes 12.

Cranberry Delight

1 cup graham cracker crumbs
¼ cup butter, melted
2 cups fresh or frozen cranberries
1 cup sugar
½ cup water
1 tsp. vanilla
⅓ cup chopped pecans
3 Tbsp. orange marmalade
1 pkg. (8 oz.) cream cheese, soft
⅓ cup powdered sugar
1 Tbsp. milk
cup heavy whipping cream, whipped

Combine crumbs and butter; press into an ungreased 8-inch square baking dish. Chill. In a sauce pan, combine cranberries, sugar and water; bring to a boil. Reduce heat and simmer for 20 minutes. Remove from the heat. Stir in pecans and marmalade; refrigerate until completely cool. Meanwhile, combine cream cheese, powdered sugar, milk and vanilla in a mixing bowl; beat until smooth. Fold in whipped cream. Spread over crust. Top with cranberry mixture. Chill for 2 hours.

Holiday Cranberry Cobbler

1 can (21 oz.) peach pie filling
1 can whole-berry cranberry sauce
1 pkg. yellow cake mix
1 tsp. cinnamon and ¼ tsp. nutmeg
1 cup cold butter
1 cup chopped nuts

Combine pie filling and cranberry sauce. Spread in an ungreased 9 x 13-inch baking dish. Combine dry cake mix & spices; cut in butter until crumbly. Stir in nuts; sprinkle over fruit. Bake at 350 degrees for 35 to 40 min. Serve warm with ice cream.

Evergreen Sandwich Cookies

Follow "Butter Cookie" Recipe (next page)
Cut out cookie with 4-inch tree shaped cookie cutter and bake per directions.

Filling: ¼ cup each shortening and butter, 2 cups powdered sugar, ½ tsp. vanilla, 4½ tsp. milk, and green paste food coloring

In a small bowl, cream the shortening, butter, and sugar until light and fluffy. Add milk and vanilla. Tint with food coloring. Spread about a tablespoon over half of the cookies; top with the remaining half of the cookies.

Glaze: 1⅓ cups powdered sugar, 4 tsp. milk, green paste food coloring and green colored sugar

Combine powdered sugar and milk until smooth; set aside ¼ cup. Stir food coloring into remaining glaze; spread thin layer over cooled cookies. If desired, sprinkle tops of half of the cookies with colored sugar. Let stand until set. If desired, pipe garland onto half of the cookies with reserved glaze. Let stand until firm.

Reproduced by Permission.
American Greetings Corporation
©AGC, LLC

Valentines Day was a special time at school when we would make fancy Valentines for our family and friends and then have a big party. It was my favorite time, because June Petek would make big heart-shaped cookies for each child. She would put our names on our own cookie. She frosted them with white frosting, then piped a fancy edge around each cookie in bright pink or red. June would make flowers or roses with leaves on one side of the cookie and our names in the middle. On extra cookies, she would write ***I Love You*** or ***Be Mine.*** They were so beautifully decorated that it was a shame to eat them. They tasted so good though, that we didn't admire them for long.

I never got June's cookie recipe but used a recipe of my grandmother's for butter cookies that tasted the same. The cookie recipe doesn't have much sugar in it, so the cookies need to be frosted for flavor. I also use the same recipe for Christmas and Halloween cookies.

I usually use two types of frosting: a thinner, creamy frosting to cover the cookie and decorator frosting for flowers and edgings. (See next page for cookie and frosting recipes.)

I made the same type of cookies for my girls when they had Valentine's parties at their school. I now understand how much work went into making all those cookies. They make heart cookie cutters in all shapes and sizes nowadays, but not back then. I once asked June how she cut out the heart cookies. She said that she would cut off the top rim of a coffee can and form it into the shape of a heart and then used that as her cookie cutter.

June Petek's talent for drawing and painting fascinated my sister, Donna, and it became a passion and a serious hobby for her. I think Donna has the talent and could pursue some kind of an art career now that her family has grown and gone. I caught the same bug about cooking and decorating cakes and cookies from June and have spent my whole life making a career out of sampling and eating my creations.

Butter Cookies *Betty Crocker's Cookbook*

1 cup soft butter
3 cups flour, sifted
½ cup sugar
½ tsp. baking powder
1 egg
3 tsp. vanilla extract

Mix butter, sugar and egg thoroughly. Stir in flavoring. Sift dry ingredients together and stir in. Chill dough. Roll out thin, about ⅛ to ¼ inch. Cut into desired shapes. Place on ungreased baking sheet. Bake until they begin to brown in a 425 degree oven for 5 to 7 minutes.

Decorator Frosting

Mix together and beat on high for about 10 minutes:

2 pounds powdered sugar
½ cup Crisco
¼ cup butter
½ cup milk, more or less
1 tsp. vanilla extract
½ tsp. almond extract

Maraschino Cherry Cake *Betty Crocker's Cookbook*

⅔ cup shortening (half butter for flavor)
1½ cups sugar
¼ cup cherry juice
¾ cup milk
16 maraschino cherries, cut in eighths
5 egg whites (⅔ cup) stiffly beaten
3 cups sifted cake flour
or 2¾ cup sifted flour
2½ tsp. baking powder
1 tsp. salt
½ cup nuts, chopped

Cream butter and sugar together until fluffy. Sift dry ingredients together. Add alternately with juice and milk. Stir in nuts and cherries. Fold in the beaten egg white. Pour into two 9-inch layer pans or a 9 x 13-inch oblong pan, greased and floured. Bake at 350 degrees for 30 to 35 minutes. Finish with cooked white frosting made with cherry juice in place of water. (see recipe below)

Fluffy White Frosting

1 cup sugar
1½ tsp. vanilla extract
2 egg whites
⅓ tsp. cream of tarter
⅓ cup water (or cherry juice)

Mix sugar, water or juice, and cream of tartar in a sauce pan. Boil slowly without stirring until syrup reaches 242 degrees. Keep saucepan covered first 3 minutes to prevent crystals from forming on sides of pan. While syrup is cooling, beat egg whites until stiff enough to hold a peak. Pour the hot syrup very slowly in a thin stream into stiffly beaten egg white, beating constantly. Add the vanilla and beat until frosting holds is shape. Spread between layers and then on cake.

Cake picture from *Wilton's Cake and Decorating Yearbook* (1970)

June Petek showed her love for children in so many ways, from parties and sleep-overs to taking us to the Vigilante Parade in Helena each year. She would show us around Helena, where she grew up, with a stop at the local candy and ice cream store, the Parrot in downtown Helena. We would also get to stop at her parents' house and visit with Grandma and Grandpa Yuhas, where there would be more fun and treats.

Connie and Cathie Petek had a special bond with their mother, June. They always had so much fun together. The love, joy and happiness they shared were extraordinary. Everyday was like Valentine's Day, as showing love just came naturally to June.

What was also amazing was the sisterly love shared between Connie and Cathie. They sang a song called "Sisters" for the Christmas program of 1955, which described the reality of their love and concern for each other. That song was so cute, and so fitting for them. The words "heaven help the Mr. who comes between me and my sister" is just an example of how protective they were and still are of each other. They have always been close and concerned for each other. They never pouted, had temper tantrums or any jealousy of each other that I have ever seen. They were not competitive or controlling. They did not have to seek attention or affirmation from others. They were not selfish, rude or nasty to each other, just kind and considerate. Well, after all these years, I finally learned their secret—Children who are loved and cared for by a warm and loving mother learn those same qualities and can then trust and care for each other.

Cathie and Connie Petek

Karleen and Donna

Cherry Cheese Pie *Country Fair Cookbook*

Graham Cracker Crumb Pie Shell: Combine ingredients in bowl and mix until crumbly:

1⅓ cup graham cracker crumbs (about 20)
¼ cup brown sugar, firmly packed
⅓ cup butter, melted

Press evenly on bottom and sides of a 9-inch pie plate

Cheese Filling:

1 (8 oz.) pkg. cream cheese
1 (3 oz.) pkg. cream cheese
2 egg whites, stiffly beaten
½ cup sugar
½ tsp. vanilla extract

Beat cream cheese (11 oz.) until light and fluffy. Blend in ½ cup sugar and vanilla. Fold in beaten egg whites. Spoon into Graham Cracker crumb pie shell.
Bake in 325 degree oven 25 minutes or until filling is set.

Cherry Topping:

1 (16 oz.) can pitted tart red cherries
Few drops red food coloring
½ teaspoon almond flavoring (optional)
¼ cup sugar
1 Tbsp. cornstarch

Drain cherries, reserving ½ cup juice. Combine cherry juice, food color, ¼ cup sugar and cornstarch in saucepan. Cook over medium heat until thick. Add almond extract. Remove from heat and cool slightly. Arrange cherries over cheese filling. Spoon sauce over top of cherries. Chill in refrigerator until serving time.

Cherry Pie

2 (16 oz.) cans pitted tart red cherries, drained or 1 quart fresh pitted red cherries
1¼ cups sugar
4 Tbsp. flour or cornstarch
¼ tsp. salt
½ tsp. almond extract
Few drops red food coloring
Pastry for a two crust 9-inch pie

Mix together sugar, flour and salt. Add cherries and stir well to coat cherries. Spoon into pastry lined pie plate. Roll remaining pastry; cut in ½-inch strips. Inter lace strips in crisscross fashion over filling to make lattice top. Trim strips even with pie edge. Turn bottom crust up over ends of strips. Press firmly to seal edge. Flute edge. Bake in 450 degree oven 10 minutes. Reduce heat to 350 degrees and bake 30 minutes or until golden brown and filling is bubbly.

Love One Another

...for love is of God

Karleen and Donna with Grandma Hammer

The unselfish type of love shown by the Peteks and many other Lincoln families can best be expressed in I Corinthians 13:4-7: "Love is very patient and kind, never jealous or envious, never boastful or proud, never haughty or selfish or rude. Love does not demand its own way. It is not irritable or touchy. It does not hold grudges and will hardly even notice when others do it wrong. It is never glad about injustice, but rejoices whenever truth wins out. If you love someone you will be loyal to him no matter what the cost. You will always believe in him, always expect the best of him, and always stand your ground in defending him." (The Living Bible, 1988, p. 1756.)

Connie and Cathie

Red Velvet Cake

2¼ cups flour, sifted
1 tsp. salt
1 cup butter
1½ cups sugar
2 eggs
1 cup buttermilk
2 Tbsp. cocoa
2 (1 oz.) bottles red food coloring (about ¼ cup)
1 tsp. vanilla extract
1 tsp. white vinegar
1 tsp. baking soda

Preheat oven to 350 degrees and grease two 9-inch cake pans. Combine the sifted flour and salt. Put the cocoa in a small glass bowl and add the food coloring gradually, stirring until smooth. Set aside. Cream together the butter and sugar, beating with electric mixer until fluffy. Beat in eggs one at a time. Keeping mixer on low speed, add flour mixture alternately with buttermilk and vanilla. Add cocoa/food coloring and mix until color of batter is uniform. Do not over beat. Mix vinegar with baking soda in a small bowl, stir briefly and fold into cake mixture. Do not beat.

Pour batter into cake pans and bake at 350 degrees for 25 to 30 minutes. Let cake cool before frosting with cream cheese or white frosting.

Frosting: Cook until thick like oatmeal and then cool: **5 Tbsp. flour** **1 cup milk**
Beat until fluffy: **1 cup butter** **1 cup granulated sugar** **1 tsp. vanilla extract**
Blend this with the cool cooked mixture and beat for several minutes:.

Chocolate Cherry Cake Donna Hammer Koss

1 box Chocolate Fudge cake mix
1 can Cherry Pie filling
1 tsp. almond extract
2 eggs

Heat oven to 350 degrees. Mix altogether and pour into a jelly roll pan. Bake for 20 to 25 minutes. Cool a little before frosting.

Frosting:
5 Tbsp. butter
1 cup sugar
⅓ cup milk
Boil this for 1 minute, then add:
6 oz. chocolate chips. Pour over cake.

No memories can compare to those of a loving grandmother. I find I think of mine more and more now that I am a grandmother and remember the kind things she did to show her love. I enjoyed spending time with her, but baking with her was the greatest. I find I still use her recipes and her first-edition *Betty Crocker's Cookbook* (1950) frequently, and especially when I bake Christmas cookies. Although she wasn't part of the Lincoln group that I grew up with, she needs to be included in this party section, since she made a party out of any event. She loved parties and always remembered birthdays and made a celebration out of them. Her specialty was a three-layer white cake with lemon filling and seven-minute frosting with coconut on top. I loved cooking with her in her large kitchen that was clean and bright with large windows and beautiful white cabinets that were hand-made by my dad. Dad built her house before we moved to Lincoln. He made cabinets for her sewing room, bathroom and utility room and even birch cabinets in the bedroom that were uniquely built like dressers.

Grandma Mehmke, my mom's mother, was probably the inventor of the "tailgate party," not for football games, but for feeding harvest crews in the fields. She didn't deliver a lunch, but a full dinner from the back end of her station wagon. Her dinners were complete with meat, potatoes and gravy, vegies, salad, dessert and fresh lemonade. She drove to the wheat fields where the men were combining and spread her feast out for their noon meal. Incidentally, that's how my parents met. My mother would help Grandma deliver dinner to the harvest crew, and my dad just happened to be working for Grandpa Mehmke.

Grandma and Grandpa Mehmke lived right off the highway between Great Falls and Belt, Montana. Many people would stop in for coffee and cookies when traveling to or from Great Falls. Grandma also liked to host "tea parties" for her garden club and church friends. She used her pretty tea sets and luncheon dishes when hosting those parties.

The men preferred her "ice cream socials" and would come in every afternoon for a treat of ice cream and cookies when working around the farm. She had a chest type freezer near the kitchen and bought ice cream in five-gallon containers from the creamery. She just opened the freezer lid and scooped it out from there, just like the ice cream parlors. She used a lot of ice cream for entertaining company, grandchildren and "the men."

Grandma and Grandpa Mehmke's house, built by Donald Hammer about 1952

Grandma had a large vegetable garden and a rose garden. She loved raising flowers and caring for her own garden and yard. She raised my mother and her brother, Carl, during the Depression years, so she knew how to stretch a dollar. She canned fruits and vegetables, raised chickens, sold eggs, milked cows and sold the extra cream and milk to help make ends meet.

Donna, Grandma Mehmke, Mom (Evelyn) and Karleen

Lemon-Filled Coconut Cake

1 cup butter, softened
2 cups sugar
3 eggs
2 tsp. vanilla extract
3¼ cups flour
3¼ tsp. baking powder
¾ tsp. salt
1½ cups milk

Filling:

1 cup sugar
¼ cup cornstarch
1 cup water
4 egg yolks, beaten
⅓ cup lemon juice
2 Tbsp. butter

Frosting:

1½ cups sugar
2 egg whites
⅓ cup water
¼ tsp. cream of tartar
1 tsp. vanilla extract
3 cups coconut, flaked

In a large bowl, cream butter and sugar until light and fluffy. Add eggs, one at a time, beating well after each addition. Beat in vanilla. Combine the dry ingredients and sift together. Add to creamed mixture alternately with milk.

Transfer to three greased and floured 9-inch round baking pans. Bake at 350 degrees for 25-30 minutes until a toothpick comes out clean. Cool in pans for 10 minutes before removing to wire racks

Filling: Combine the sugar, cornstarch and water in a small saucepan, stirring until smooth. Bring to a boil, cook and stir 2 minutes longer or until thick and bubbly. Remove from heat. Stir a small amount of hot mixture into egg yolks, return all to pan, stirring constantly. Bring to a gentle boil; cook and stir 2 minutes longer. Remove from heat; gently stir in lemon juice and butter. Cool to room temperature without stirring. Place one cake on serving plate; spread with half of the filling. Repeat layers. Top with remaining cake.

The Mehmke Family—Marguerite, Walter, Evelyn and Carl

Frosting: Combine the sugar, egg whites, water and cream of tartar in a large heavy saucepan. With a portable mixer, beat on low speed for 1 minute. Continue beating over low heat until frosting reaches 160 degrees, about 10 minutes. Transfer to a large bowl; add vanilla. Beat on high until stiff peaks form, about 7 minutes. Frost top and sides of cake. Sprinkle with coconut.

Fresh Orange Cake

Follow the above recipe for lemon-filled cake—*except* omit vanilla and add **2 tsp. orange extract** for flavoring and add **2 tsp. grated orange rind** to batter. Bake in layers as above, but put together with Rich Orange Filling. Frost the top and sides as above, with or without coconut.

Rich Orange Filling:

Follow the above recipe for lemon filling *except* omit water and use **1 cup orange juice and 2 Tbsp. grated orange rind**. Reduce the lemon juice to 2 Tbsp. For a clear Orange Filling, omit the egg yolks.

After Grandpa Mehmke semi-retired from farming, he began collecting and restoring steam engines. He made friends from all over the United States as he gathered parts for the engines. There wasn't e-mail or internet back then, so there were a lot of phone calls and letters written to communicate with other collectors around the country to find the right parts. He began hosting an annual "threshing bee," where large crowds would gather to watch as he and many of his friends would run the steam engines, threshing equipment, plows and drills. It took many men to keep the boilers loaded with wood or coal, which was a hot and dirty job. Of course, Grandma figured all those people needed to be fed, but there was no way she could keep up, as each year the crowds increased in size. Her church friends and other civic groups soon came to her aid and turned the garage into a hamburger/hotdog stand. The "Threshing Bee" became quite a fund-raiser for various groups, organizations and vendors. Of course, Grandma always kept the house open to all the wives who came along. They enjoyed visiting where it was cool and a bit quieter. Grandma supported Grandpa's new hobby and traveled with him to various parts of the country as he shopped for steam engines and parts for them. I don't know how many he finally ended up with, but they filled two huge sheds behind his shop and garage.

Grandpa Walter Mehmke

Proverbs 31: 23,24 "Her husband is well known for he sits in the council chamber with the other civic leaders. She makes belted linen garments to sell to the merchants."

After Grandpa died in 1976, his only son, Carl took over the steam engine collection, and it soon became his hobby as he continued the tradition. Carl died in 2009, leaving the collection to his daughters, Charlotte and Mardel, and son, Walter Jr.

Since my mother and uncle Carl were the only two children Grandma and Grandpa had, they had more time and energy to focus on only five grandchildren—my sister, Donna, myself and our cousins, Walter, Charlotte and Mardel.

Grandpa Mehmke with Donna, Charlotte, Karleen and Walter on Christmas Eve shopping trip.

Mom (Evelyn) with Carl and Martha Mehr

MEHMKE'S GAVE A PARTY

Mehmke's gave a party.
The folks by hundreds came,
They came to see the steam engines
Thresh the golden grain;
To thrill at sights they had not seen
Since many years ago,
Or maybe never in their life
Had they heard steam whistles blow
They came to see the Giants
That broke the virgin sod
Once again strain their power
Against the hard-packed clod.
To see the flywheel flying,
And hear the pistons hiss,
For once one has heard it,
The call can never miss.

Carl Mehmke

Grandpa Mehmke

Mehmke's gave a party
The crowds by thousands came,
They came from out the city
& cross the wide, wide plain,
They came clear down from Canada
From Oregon & West
Clear up from California
Yearning for the zest
The call of the steam whistle
Draws from far and near
For many, Mehmke's Threshing Bee
is a high-light of the year.

When Mehmke's give a party
They have the Highway Patrol
Just to handle parking,
That's their only role
And the Sheriff's Posse
In case the cops should fail
For the cars come by thousands
To the engines wail.
To smell the smell of coal smoke,
For once it's in your blood,
You never can remove it,
No matter how you tug
If once, you've heard the whistle
You just have to go
So come join the happy thousands
At Mehmke's Threshing Show.

Grandpa and Karleen (1960)

by John D. Ellingsen
September 11, 1966
♡H

Tina Robinson '84

Grandma and Grandpa made yearly trips to Texas and Arizona. When they came home, the car was filled with oranges, lemons, grapefruit, dates, raisins and nuts. They were able to buy them fresh and locally grown. In order to use up all the fruit, Grandma baked many goodies out of lemons, oranges and dates. Grandpa's favorite cookies were oatmeal raisin cookies and anything that had dates in them. Therefore, that is what we baked with until the supply ran out.

When Donna and I would stay with our grandparents, Grandma Mehmke would help us bake and sew but our favorite thing was to play with paper dolls. She would save her Sears and Montgomery Wards catalogs for us to cut up for doll cloths and decorate rooms in our paper houses for the paper dolls. We would cut and play for hours.

Grandma was the person who always came to the rescue when things weren't going right. She didn't brush things under the rug and hope they would just go away. She tackled problems head on. We stayed with her a lot as children, partly because we loved to be there during the summers. Our mother suffered from periods of severe depression at times throughout her life. Grandma could tell when things were not as they should be. She would come and get us kids and get Mom the medical help she needed. When I came down with polio, I can still remember how sick I was, unable to move and lying with my head over the edge of the bed vomiting frequently. Mom must have called Grandma for help, for as soon as she arrived, I knew things were about to happen as she scooped me up and got me to the hospital.

When we would stay with Grandma during the summer months, our cousins, Walter, Charlotte and Mardel would frequently come to her house to play with us. They just lived across the highway from Grandma and Grandpa, as Uncle Carl and Grandpa farmed together. Grandma was always fearful of rattlesnakes and warned us not to go too far or into the tall grass when we went outside to play. One morning as we were going out to play in the yard, Grandma heard the sound of a rattler. The snake was just beneath the big cottonwood tree where we were headed. She made us all get back into the house, and out of nowhere she appeared with a shotgun in hand and shot that old snake to smithereens.

Along with being loving and protective of children, I learned many other valuable lessons from Grandma about cooking and cleanliness. Some of Grandma's rules were:

1. Always prepare enough food just in case somebody extra shows up at mealtime.
2. Don't throw food away or waste food. Save leftovers for soups, potpies or stew.
3. Save the water used to cook vegetables and potatoes as it is high in nutrients such as potassium that shouldn't go down the drain. Use the water for gravy or soups. Save potato cooking water for making bread.

4. Use vegetable oils for baking, when possible, and for frying instead of solid shortening. She understood the principle about hydrogenated shortenings. In short, her philosophy was that if it doesn't melt at room temperature or body temperature, then what does it do once in the body besides collect in arteries.
5. Butter is natural, flavorful and safer to use than margarine and other hydrogenated shortenings. People who work hard and burn calories need fat in their diet to supply the body with fuel after the carbohydrates (sugars) have been used up and burned off. She also said, "If God made it, then use it."

Date Filled Cookies

½ cup soft shortening
1 cup sugar
2 eggs
2½ cups flour
¼ tsp. baking soda
½ tsp. salt
2 Tbsp. thick cream
1 tsp. vanilla extract

Cream shortening, sugar and eggs. Add cream and vanilla. Sift and add all dry ingredients to creamed mixture. Chill dough at least 1 hour. Roll out ¼ inch thick and cut 3 inch rounds and place on cookie sheet. Place a rounded teaspoon full of cooled date filling on each. Top with another cookie round and press edges together. Pierce with a fork in center over filled portion of cookie or cut out a small hole to display the filling. Bake at 400 degrees for 8 to 10 minutes.

Date Filling

1½ cups dates (can also use raisins and/or figs)
½ cup water
½ cup sugar
2 Tbsp. lemon juice

Cook slowly; stir until thickened, about 5 minutes. Cool before placing in cookie.

Date Cranberry Orange Bars

½ cup margarine, softened
1 cup sugar, divided
1⅓ cups flour, divided
3 eggs
1 pkg. (8 oz.) pitted dates, cut up or chopped
½ cup dried cranberries
¼ cup orange juice

Beat margarine and ½ cup sugar, in bowl, until light and creamy. Stir in 1 cup flour. Press onto bottom of 8 or 9- inch square pan. Bake at 375 degrees, 12 to 15 minutes or until edges start to brown. Beat eggs in bowl, stir in remaining sugar, flour, dates, cranberries and juice. Pour over crust. Bake 20 minutes more or until lightly browned. Sprinkle with powdered sugar, if desired. Cut into bars.

Date Bars

Filling: **1 cup dates, packed** **1 cup water** **1 cup sugar**

Boil for 15 minutes, then simmer until soft.

Crust:

2½ cups quick oatmeal **1 cup brown sugar, packed** **2 cups flour**
¾ cup shortening **1 tsp. soda dissolved in 1 Tbsp. hot water**
1 tsp. vanilla Mix the above ingredients together with a pastry blended. Use half the crumb mixture on bottom of a 9 x 13-inch pan. Spread date filling evenly to sides. Pat rest of crumbled mixture evenly on top. Bake 350 degrees for 25 to 30 minutes.

Date Marshmallow Log

30 Graham crackers, crushed
1 cup chopped dates
16 large marshmallows, cut up
or ⅓ lb. miniature marshmallows
2 cups walnuts, broken
1 cup whipping cream

Combine all dry ingredients. Mix in the cream (not whipped) well. Shape into roll 3 inches across. Wrap in waxed paper, chill in refrigerator. To serve, cut into slices. Garnish with whipped cream.

Grandpa Walter Mehmke with granddaughters Karleen and Donna Hammer

6. Don't throw away food scraps. All fruit and vegetable peelings, eggshells and coffee grounds can go to a compost pile. Meat scraps should be fed to dogs or cats. Turkey carcasses and bones can be cooked for soup broth, but throw the bones away instead of feeding to animals as they can splinter and get stuck in the animal's intestines.
7. "Cleanliness is next to Godliness." Grandma was a stickler for hand washing. She had a sink near the back door where the men and kids washed up before coming into the house or kitchen. She didn't appreciate hand washing in her kitchen sink or "the men" in her cooking area in the kitchen with their dirty clothes on. She had a large table in an area away from the main kitchen where they would visit and wait for her to serve them. Her house and kitchen were always clean and she used lots of hot water, soap and elbow grease to keep them that way.
8. Grandma instructed us to "read your Bible every day and pray often throughout the day." *Psalm 119: 105 "Thy word is a lamp unto my feet and a light unto my path."*
9. Grandma had many other tidbits for working hard and saving, but the best thing she taught us was to trust and respect the Lord. *Proverbs 2; 1, 7 "Every young person who listens to me and obeys my instructions will be given wisdom and good sense." "His every word (the Bible) is a treasure of knowledge and understanding."*

I still cherish the famous pictures that my grandmother gave me by Warner Sallman that depict the quiet strength complete peace and loving compassion on Jesus' face, similar to what I saw in my grandmother's face.

Grandma Marguerite Mehmke

Four Generations-Grandma Ber Grandma Mehmke, Evelyn (Mom and baby Karleen Hammer

Grandma Mehmke with Mom (Evelyn) and Mardel

Hot Lemonade or Tea

3 cups water or tea
¾ cup lemon juice
1½ tsp. lemon peel, grated
⅔ cup sugar
4 cinnamon sticks, opt.

In a saucepan over medium heat, simmer water or tea, lemon juice, sugar and lemon peel until sugar is dissolved. Serve with a cinnamon stick if desired.

Chai Tea

1 cup powdered milk
1 cup creamer
1 cup French vanilla creamer
1½ cups sugar
2 Tbsp. pumpkin pie spice
1½ cups instant tea

Mix all the ingredients together and blend one cup at a time in a blender to a fine powder. Store in an airtight container. Add about 2 to 3 tablespoons to warm milk or hot water.

Christmas Tea

9 cups boiling water
1 cup sugar
2 Tbsp. instant tea
⅔ cup lemon juice
1 tsp. almond extract
1 tsp. vanilla extract

Combine all ingredients and serve

Grandma Mehmke dwarfed by an Avery steam engine

Russian Tea

2 cups powdered Tang
1 cup sugar
1 cup Lipton tea (instant) with lemon
1 tsp. each of cloves and cinnamon

Mix together in a large bowl. Place dry mix in jars or container store. Add about 3 teaspoons to 1 cup hot water, or to taste.

Grandma Mehmke also had some rules for making and serving tea that still apply today. She would fill the glass teapot with boiling water to heat up the pot before using it to brew tea. She would then heat up another tea kettle of water to boiling, dump the warm water out of the tea pot and fill with fresh hot water. She used one tea bag for every 1 to 2 cups of water in the pot and let it steep for 5 to 10 minutes. She always had cookies baked ahead and in the freezer for unexpected guests. She collected beautiful dishes and wasn't afraid to use them for her guests. I have some of her tea sets in my possession, but they are antiques now.

My Grandmother Mehmke was also a great seamstress, as was my mother. Grandma taught my mother, Evelyn, to sew at a very young age. Since there wasn't TV or computers in those days, the favorite pastime for girls was to sew, read or do needlework.

My Mother had very poor eyesight and claimed it was because she did so much embroidery and reading in dim lights as a child. Electricity wasn't always available, so kerosene lamps and candles were the old standby for lighting on long winter evenings. Mother claimed eating carrots (because of the vitamin A content) would prevent serious vision problems. So needless to say, carrots in any shape or form became one of her specialties. As I look at old family photos, I see glasses being worn by all the Mehmke clan with Grandpa's German heritage, but not so with Grandma's Norwegian family. Could there be something to genetics and vision problems after all?

Mother's sewing skills have always been her greatest gift. I loved the matching dresses and coats she would make for my sister Donna and I. She also made cute curtains and drapes for our house and even did some furniture upholstery work. She told us that aprons were what she made when first learning to sew. Aprons then became the first projects Donna and I learned to sew as well. By the time I started teaching my daughters to sew, aprons were out of style. My oldest daughter, Karla, still got the old apron sewing start though. She is an accomplished seamstress and quilter now. My youngest daughter's first projects were nightgowns for her sisters' Christmas gifts. I even got one of her handmade flannel nightgowns, but as I look at it, I wonder if I could ever fit into it again.

My Mother also helped sew the costumes for the Christmas program of 1955. My choir robe wasn't hard to sew, but Donna's bunny outfit was a challenge. She helped other mothers sew their children's outfits also. *Proverbs 31: 21, 22 "She has no fear of winter for her household, for she has made warm clothes for all of them. She also upholsters with finest tapestry. Her own clothing is beautifully made—a purple gown of pure linen."*

Donna and Karleen Hammer wearing the frilly dresses that were sewn for us with love by our mother (Evelyln). We even wore matching homemade wool coats.

Carrot Cookies

Evelyn Hammer
Old Lincoln Cookbook

1 cup cooked mashed carrots or 2 cups raw grated carrots
¾ cup shortening
¾ cup sugar
1 egg
1 tsp. vanilla extract
2 tsp. baking powder
½ cup nuts or coconut
2 cups flour
½ tsp. salt

Cream shortening, sugar, egg, and vanilla. Add sifted dry ingredients. Add carrots and nuts. Drop by teaspoon on greased cookie sheet. Bake at 375 degrees for 12 to 15 minutes.

Orange Butter Icing

3 Tbsp. soft butter
1½ cups powdered sugar
2 tsp. grated orange peel
Juice of 1 orange (about 1 Tbsp.)

Blend sugar and butter. Stir in orange peel and juice. Beat until frosting is smooth and of spreading consistency.

Classic Carrot and Pineapple Cake

1 cup crushed pineapple, drained
1½ cups cooking oil
2 cups sugar
3 eggs
2 cups grated carrots
2½ cups sifted flour
1 tsp. baking soda
½ tsp. salt
1½ tsp. cinnamon
1 tsp. vanilla extract

Cream oil, sugar and eggs; add pineapple and grated carrots. Mix well. Sift flour, soda, salt and cinnamon together, then add to to creamed mixture; add vanilla. Beat well. Bake 45 minutes at 350 degrees.

Cream Cheese Frosting

1 (3 oz.) cream cheese
1 Tbsp. milk
2 cups or more powdered sugar
1 stick butter
1 tsp. vanilla extract

Beat first 4 ingredients until creamy. Add powdered sugar until smooth. Top with chopped nuts.

Carrot Oatmeal Cookies

1 cup butter, softened
1 cup shortening
1½ cups sugar
1½ cups brown sugar
4 eggs
2 tsp. vanilla extract
2 tsp. salt
3½ cups flour
2 tsp. baking soda
1 cup chopped walnuts
1 cup raisins
4 cups quick cooking oats
2 cups carrots, shredded

In a large mixing bowl, cream the butter, shortening and sugars. Beat in the eggs and vanilla. Add carrots; mix well. Combine the flour, soda and salt; add to the creamed mixture and mix well. Stir in the walnut, oats and raisins. Cover and refrigerate for at least 4 hours. Drop by rounded tablespoonfuls 3 inches apart onto baking sheets coated with cooking spray. Bake at 375 degrees for 10 to 13 minutes or until lightly browned. Cool for 2 minutes before removing to wire racks.

Back to aprons—I saw this commentary in the *Blackfoot Valley Dispatch* awhile back about aprons that so reminded me of my grandmother and my mother.

History of Aprons

I don't think our kids know what an apron is. The principal use of Grandma's apron was to protect the dress underneath, but along with that, it served as a potholder for removing hot pans from the oven.

It was wonderful for drying children's tears, and on occasion was even used for cleaning out dirty ears. From the chicken coop, the apron was used for carrying eggs, fuzzy chicks, and sometimes a half-hatched egg to be finished in the warming oven.

When company came, those aprons were ideal hiding places for shy kids. And when the weather was cold, Grandma wrapped it around her arms.

Those big old aprons wiped many a perspiring brow, bent over the hot wood stove. Chips and kindling wood were brought into the kitchen in that apron.

From the garden it carried all sorts of vegetables. After the peas had been shelled, it carried out the hulls.

In the fall, the apron was used to bring in apples that had fallen from the trees. When unexpected company drove up the road, it was surprising how much furniture that old apron could dust in a matter of seconds.

When dinner was ready, Grandma walked out onto the porch, waved her apron, and the men knew it was time to come in from the fields to dinner.

It will be a long time before someone invents something that will replace that "old-time apron" that served so many purposes.

Remember: Grandma used to set her baked apple pies on the windowsill to cool. Her granddaughters set theirs on the windowsill to thaw. They would go crazy now trying to figure out how many germs were on that apron. I don't think I ever caught anything from an apron. (BVD Smile File, February, 2009)

Aprons, just like home cooking, are now coming back into style. There are such neat patterns and fabrics now days which help make it fun to sew and create beautiful things. My mom hasn't got the quilting bug yet, but my sister has and she makes gorgeous gifts. With our bad economy, maybe homemade gifts like cookies, candies, aprons and quilts will come back into style again.

I realize that I must begin to wind up this section about parties, especially birthday parties and the mothers who put them on. I always wanted a party of my own, but since we didn't have a home of our own, my mother was reluctant to have one.

Pecan-Topped Carrot Pie

4 cups fresh sliced carrots
2 eggs
¼ tsp. ground cinnamon
1 tsp. pumpkin pie spice
1 can (14 oz.) sweetened condensed milk
Dash salt
1 unbaked pastry shell (9 inches)
½ cup packed brown sugar
3 Tbsp. butter, melted
1 cup chopped pecans

Add 1 inch of water to a large saucepan; add carrots. Bring to a boil. Reduce heat; cover and cook for 9 to 11 minutes or until carrots are tender. Drain and cool.

Place carrots, eggs, milk, pie spice, cinnamon and salt in a blender. Cover and process until pureed; process 1 minute longer. Pour into pastry shell.

Combine the pecans, brown sugar and butter; sprinkle over filling.

Bake at 375 degrees for 45-50 minutes or until a knife inserted near the center comes out clean and the edges are browned. (Cover the edges of crust with foil during the last 20 minutes to prevent over browning if necessary.)

Orange Coconut Meringue Pie

1 cup sugar
3 Tbsp. cornstarch
3 Tbsp. flour
¼ tsp. salt
1½ cups water
¾ cup orange juice
3 egg yolks, lightly beaten
¾ cup flaked coconut
1 Tbsp. grated orange peel
2 Tbsp. butter
2 Tbsp. lemon juice
1 pastry shell (9-inch) baked

In a large saucepan, combine sugar, cornstarch, flour and salt. Gradually stir in water and orange juice until smooth. Cook and stir over medium-high heat until thickened and bubbly. Reduce the heat; cook and stir 2 minutes longer. Remove from the heat.

Stir a small amount of hot filling into egg yolks, return all to the pan, stirring constantly. Bring to a gentle boil, cook and stir 2 minutes longer. Remove from the heat. Stir in the coconut, butter and orange peel. Gently stir in lemon juice. Pour into pastry shell.

Meringue:

3 egg whites
½ tsp. vanilla extract
¼ tsp. cream of tartar
6 Tbsp. sugar

In a small bowl, beat egg whites, vanilla and cream of tartar on medium speed until soft peaks form. Gradually beat in sugar, 1 tablespoon at a time, on high until stiff glossy peaks form and sugar is dissolved. Spread evenly over hot filling, sealing edges to crust. Bake at 350 degrees for 12 to 15 minutes, or until the meringue is golden brown. Cool on a wire wire rack hour. Refrigerate for 3 hours before serving.

Pineapple Meringue Pie

1 cup sugar
4 Tbsp. cornstarch
1 cup pineapple juice
½ cup hot water
3 egg yolks, slightly beaten
1¼ cup well drained pineapple
1½ tsp. grated lemon rind
1 Tbsp. lemon juice
3 Tbsp. butter

Mix sugar and cornstarch in a saucepan. Gradually stir in pineapple juice and hot water. Cook over medium heat, stirring constantly, until mixture thickens and boils. Boil 1 minute. Beat a little of the hot mixture into the egg yolks. Then beat into the hot mixture in saucepan. Boil 1 minute longer, stirring constantly until smooth. Blend in the butter, lemon juice and rind and drained pineapple. Pour into a baked 9-inch pie shell. Cover with meringue. Bake until a delicate brown.

Meringue: Follow the recipe above for ingredients and baking instructions

My mother was never too thrilled about moving to Lincoln and leaving her home in Great Falls, or her parents. Dad's new career of building log homes and lodges in and around the Lincoln area was a new adventure for him. His type of logs and buildings were coming into demand, and he was no longer able to commute to and from Great Falls to do all the jobs he was getting in Lincoln. He had already moved his log peeling operation from his garage in our back yard in Great Falls to his new shop across from the 7-Up Ranch. He bought the land next to the sawmill from his employer in Great Falls (Pappin Construction) who helped him get his operation started. We lived in the McClure house the first summer, but we had to go back to Great Falls so I could start school and mother could get back to her new log home in the city.

We moved up to Lincoln again the next summer, and Donna and I were able to start school in Lincoln in the fall. We moved into a small trailer in the trailer park by Lambkin's Hotel. The Lambkin's were good to us and gave my dad his first big job in Lincoln, which was building Lambkin's Bar and Restaurant.

I loved living in that little trailer among those huge pine trees. It was a short walk to school and close to our new friends, Connie and Cathie Petek at Stoner's Store, Mary Grosfield at the end of Sleepy Hollow Road and Claudia Wildin, whose family lived across the street above the little Phillips 66 station.

The movie *The Long, Long Trailer* with Lucille Ball and Desi Arnez was popular then. It was a hilarious movie to watch. I still laugh when I think about that movie and living in that little trailer. Mobile homes, about the size of today's campers, were just coming into style back then. I thought that little trailer was the neatest thing ever and we were "right up town" until winter came.

Dad had just finished a log summer home for the Johnson's from Great Falls on a then isolated little roadway that is now the North Airport Road. We moved into it for the winter and stayed warm and cozy as he finished up the interior work and built kitchen cabinets. Donna and I had so much fun playing in the snow and sledding out there. We were late to school at times as we would have to wait for the road to get plowed. This prompted Dad to invest in his first little D3ACcrawler so he could keep the road plowed. Mother seemed to do well with the solitude out there and had fun sewing and baking in that new house.

The original Johnson cabin painted by Donna Hammer Koss

That spring, we moved into town and rented a small house near to where Dad was building a log cabin for the Zadicks from Great Falls on First Avenue. That house we rented is now owned by Phyllis Wells and her husband Jack Ward. It was very small then, but they have turned it into a beautiful and much larger home. Dad bought three lots across from the Zadick cabin, one for our new home and two for spec homes he hoped to build at a later time.

The original Zadick cabin as seen from our living room window which shows the basic style of Don Hammer's log homes.

Donald Hammer's first crawler is now a part of the Mehmke Steam Engine and Tractor Museum

Orange Slice Pineapple Fruitcake

1 cup orange candy slices, chopped
1 cup candied cherries, chopped
1 cup pecans, chopped
1 cup candied pineapple, chopped
2 cups flour, divided
2 cups butter, soft **2 cups sugar**
6 eggs **2 tsp. vanilla**
1 tsp. baking powder

In bowl, combine the candy, cherries, pineapple, pecans and 1 cup flour; set aside. In a mixing bowl, cream butter and sugar. Add eggs, one at a time beating well after each. Beat in vanilla. Combine baking powder and remaining flour; gradually add to creamed mixture. Fold in fruit mixture. Spoon into a greased and waxed paper-lined 10-inch tube pan. Bake at 300 degrees for 1¾ to 2 hours or until a toothpick inserted near the center comes out clean. Cool for 10 minutes before removing from pan to a wire rack. Remove waxed paper while warm; cool completely before cutting into slices.

Orange Angel Delight

Dissolve **1 package of orange Jello in 1 cup of boiling water**. Add **1 cup of orange juice with pulp, the juice of ½ lemon and ¾ cup sugar**. Cook until it starts to thicken. Whip **1 cup of cream** and add to Jello mixture and stir well. Break an **angel food cake** into small pieces covering the bottom of a large cake pan. Cover the cake with **2 cups of miniature marshmallows and ¾ cup chopped nuts**. Pour Jello mixture over all and let stand in refrigerator until firm.

Old Fashioned Butterscotch Pie

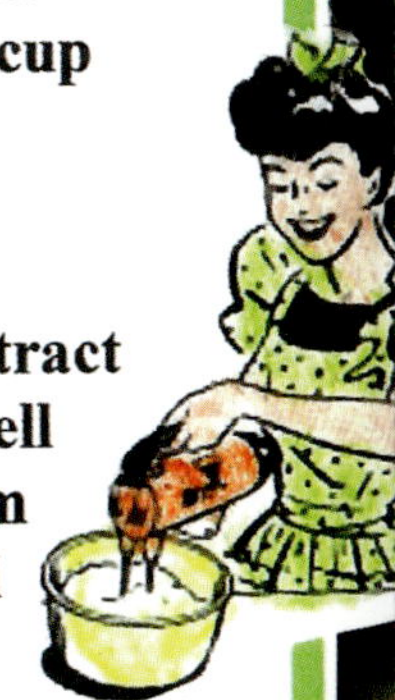

½ cup butter or margarine
1 cup brown sugar, firmly packed
1 cup boiling water
3 Tbsp. cornstarch
2 Tbsp. flour
¾ tsp. salt
1½ cups milk
4 egg yolks, slightly beaten
1½ tsp. vanilla extract
1 baked 9" pie shell
1 cup heavy cream
½ tsp. vanilla and
1 Tbsp. sugar

Brown butter in heavy saucepan over low heat. Stir in brown sugar and boiling water. Bring to a boil; boil 2 minutes, stirring constantly. Combine cornstarch, flour and salt. Gradually stir in milk; mix until smooth. Stir into brown sugar mixture. Cook, stirring constantly, until mixture comes to a boil and thickens, about 5 to 7 minutes. Stir a little of the hot mixture into egg yolks; blend well. Gradually stir all of egg yolk mixture into cooked custard; Blend well. Cook 1 minute, stirring constantly. Remove from heat. Stir in 1½ tsp. vanilla. Cool well. Pour filling into pie shell and chill. Whip heavy cream with ½ tsp. vanilla and 1 Tbsp. sugar until soft peaks form. Serve topped with the whipped cream topping, or a meringue would also work.

Pineapple Fluff Cake

Bernice Lambkin in *The Old Lincoln Cookbook*

Beat **6 egg whites** and **¼ tsp. salt** until peaks form. Then beat **6 egg yolks** and **¾ cup sugar** until light yellow and creamy. Add **½ cup pineapple juice** and **1 tsp. lemon juice** to egg yolk mixture and beat. Sift together **1½ cup cake flour** and **1 tsp. baking powder** and add to egg yolk mixture. Fold in stiffly beaten whites; pour into a 10-inch angel food pan. Bake at 325 degrees for 1 hour.

So my mother finally got the house she was promised for packing up and leaving Great Falls and her family to move to God's country. Living and growing up in Lincoln always seemed like a party to me because of all the loving and helpful people in the community. Grandma Mehmke always said that God is everywhere we are, but I always feel His presence more in Lincoln, walking in fresh air among those magnificent trees.

I finally got my birthday party in our new house. What a delight. Birthday parties are such an important event for children. Making a big fuss over them is something that will always be remembered. Whether it is held in a tent or a house, it doesn't matter as long as a little child feels loved and special.

It was so much fun looking through old family slides for these special photos. I knew there were some pictures someplace of that special party. It must have been my twelfth birthday in February 1959. I am not sure who all the girls are in the photos, but the girls facing forward are: Claudia Wildin behind the white cake with her hand up, Vonnie Barns at the far end of the table, Diana Welch, Phyllis Wells and Terry Routzahn at the back of the table, Becky Youdarian standing in the red skirt and Mary Grosfield seated at the near end of the table next to me. I am the one with the skinny left arm wearing my new homemade dress. My mother is in the background wearing her apron that kind of matches my dress. My sister, Donna, and Connie and Cathie Petek, must have been seated at the counter off to the left.

Chiffon Cake

Betty Crocker's Cookbook

½ cup vegetable oil
7 egg yolks, unbeaten
¼ cup cold water
2 tsp. vanilla extract
2 tsp. lemon rind, grated

2 cups sifted flour
1½ cup sugar
3 tsp. baking powder
1 tsp. salt
1 cup egg whites (7 to 8)
½ tsp. cream of tartar

Sift dry ingredients in a bowl. "Make a well" in flour and add all first 5 ingredients in order as listed above. Whip egg whites and cream of tartar in a large mixing bowl until whites form very stiff peaks. Pour egg yolk mixture gradually over whipped whites, gently folding with rubber scraper just until blended. Pour into ungreased 10-inch tube pan or 9 x 13-inch oblong pan. Bake 10-inch tube pan at 325 degrees for 55 minutes, then at 350 degrees for 10 to 15 minutes. Bake oblong cake at 350 degrees for 50 to 55 minutes. When cake tests done, invert and let hang until cold.

Pineapple Chiffon Cake

Follow recipe above except use **pineapple juice** in place of water. Add to "well", **½ cup well drained finely crushed pineapple.** (See pineapple frosting recipe below).

Orange Chiffon Cake

Follow recipe above except omit vanilla and lemon rind. Add **3 Tbsp. grated orange rind. Orange juice** may be used in place of water. Finish with Orange Butter Icing.

Champion Sponge Cake

1¼ cup sifted flour
1 cup sugar
½ tsp. baking powder
½ tsp. salt
6 eggs, separated

1 tsp. cream of tartar
½ cup sugar
¼ cup water
1 tsp. vanilla extract

Sift together flour, 1 cup sugar, baking powder and salt.
Beat egg whites at high speed until frothy. Add cream of tartar. Gradually add ½ cup sugar, beating until stiff.
Combine egg yolks, water, vanilla and dry ingredients. Beat at medium-high speed until thick and lemon-colored (about 4 minutes).
Gradually fold egg yolk mixture into egg whites. Pour batter into ungreased 10-inch tube pan. Bake in 350 degree oven 45 minutes or until cake tests done. Invert tube pan on funnel or bottle to cool. When completely cooled, remove from pan.

Pineapple Frosting

Cream together **¼ cup butter and ¼ cup shortening.**
Gradually add **3 cups sifted powdered sugar;** beat until light and fluffy.
Stir in **1 (8½ oz.) can drained crushed pineapple, ⅛ tsp. salt, ¼ tsp. vanilla extract and ½ tsp. lemon rind.**

The greatest thing finally happened in my little world back in 1958. The Petek family moved into a little two-story cabin style house at the end of our lane where First Avenue now joins with "C" Street. It wasn't such a good year for the Peteks, though, as they had to give up Stoner's Store in order to pay back creditors. Johnny Petek had a good heart and extended credit to customers who never paid him back. He said he just couldn't let anybody go hungry, especially during the winter months. Johnny Petek continued running his propane delivery service truck and the garage after they moved out of the cute little house on the back of Stoner's Store.

It was wonderful having the Peteks living just a block away from our house. We were able to do more and more fun things with them. Connie and I did lots of baking projects and experimental cooking together. Connie can still remember the time we tried to make potato chips. I don't think we ever repeated that one ever again, and you certainly won't see our recipe in this cookbook.

Cathie Petek and my sister, Donna were horseback riding buddies then. Before the Bossings moved to First Avenue and built their chicken barns, the area west of the street was vacant and unfenced. There was and still is, a huge field where we used to ride bikes, walk or ride horses along a little road that headed west from First Avenue, followed along near the river through the field and then into the trees. That little road went west of town to where Brent and Carla Anderson's home is now. There used to be a sawmill and pond there at one time. That roadway also continued further west to where the Thompson's had a sawmill. The little roadway then turned northward, went through Thompson's and then joined Highway 200. That roadway was also a favorite spot for fisherman, since the Blackfoot River runs so close along there. It was also a great route to the Youderian place which was then just a few miles west of town. The Youderians leased the Zimbleman place for some years before they bought their own ranch up Beaver Creek Road. We spent a lot of time riding with the Youderian girls, Becky and Marty. That little roadway was a safer way to get to the Youderians, avoiding all the traffic out on Highway 200.

I believe that ranch is now owned by the Crys, who are related to the Zimblemans, the original owners, who bought the land from Len Lambkin way back when.

Donna Hammer and Cathie Petek

I don't know who owned that field back then, which was next to the house the Peteks rented, but there was never any problem for kids or fisherman to travel along it. My dad could walk from our house down that road to his favorite fishing hole. It was also his favorite place to pull us on a toboggan with his pickup in the winter time. Donna and Cathie spent many hours riding bikes and horses to and from the Youderians along their little secret roadway.

Elegant Desserts

Triple Layer Dessert *The Lincoln Cookbook*

Crust:

1 stick margarine **1¼ cup flour**

Cut margarine into flour until crumbly. Press into bottom of 9 x 13-inch pan and bake 5 minutes at 350 degrees. Cool.

Second Layer:

1 (8 oz.) pkg. cream cheese **1 cup powdered sugar**
7 oz. Cool Whip

Beat powdered sugar into softened cream cheese until fluffy. Fold in Cool Whip until smooth. Spread over crust.

Third Layer:

2 (3 oz.) pkgs. "instant" pudding--chocolate, pistachio, lemon or butterscotch flavor **3 cups cold milk**

Beat until thick (almost 3 minutes) and spread over second layer. Top with **7 oz. Cool Whip and finely chopped walnuts.** Cool in refrigerator for 2 hours

Classic Cheesecake

Crumb Crust:

11 whole graham crackers **¼ cup melted butter** **2 Tbsp. sugar**

Preheat oven to 325 degrees. Crush graham crackers into crumbs. Add the butter and sugar, and mix. Press into the base of a 9-inch springform pan. Chill.

Filling:

5 pkg. (8 oz. each) cream cheese
1½ cups sugar
3 Tbsp. flour
3 large eggs
½ cup sour cream
2 tsp. finely grated lemon peel
1½ tsp. vanilla extract

Place the cream cheese in a large bowl. Beat on medium-high speed for 2 minutes. Blend in the sugar. Add the flour and beat until combined. On low speed, beat in the eggs, one at a time, just until blended. Add the sour cream, lemon peel and vanilla and beat until blended. Pour the filling over the crust in the pan. Bake the cheesecake for 1 hour and 15 minutes. Turn off oven and keep the oven door ajar. Let the cheesecake sit in oven for 1 hour. Transfer to a wire rack to cool completely. Run a knife around sides. Cover; chill for 6 hours or overnight. Top with canned fruit or fresh fruit pie filling (cherry, blueberry).

Cream Pie Fillings Dorothy Andersons' *Memories of Mom Cookbook*

1 cup sugar
½ tsp. salt
2½ Tbsp. cornstarch
1 Tbsp. flour
3 cups milk
3 egg yolks, beaten
1 tbsp. butter
1½ tsp. vanilla

Mix dry ingredients in saucepan. Gradually stir in milk. Cook over moderate heat, stirring constantly, until mixture thickens and boils. Boil 1 minute. Remove from heat. Stir a little of the milk mixture into the egg yolks; then blend into the hot mixture in saucepan. Boil 1 minute, stirring constantly. Remove from heat and stir in butter and vanilla. Cool then pour into a baked pie shell. Chill thoroughly. Cover with whipped cream.

Chocolate Cream Pie: Add **3 Tbsp. cocoa** to sugar mixture.

Banana Cream Pie: Arrange a layer of **sliced bananas** in pastry shell; add cooled filling.

After the Peteks moved from that house, Pauline and Leonard Orr moved in and Donna then had another horseback riding partner, Betty Jean Orr. Those girls spent so much time riding around that area that Leonard Orr named First Avenue "Horse Shit Lane."

Whenever I would walk or drive by that little house, I could still remember all the warmth and fun and laughter that happened there.

There was a real rock fireplace that kept the living room so cozy and inviting. June was a great hostess and held many parties and events there. We also had Girls Scout meetings and confirmation classes there along with the many parties.

Connie and I baked lots of cookies in that house. We loved to watch June decorate her beautiful cookies and cakes at the neat little home. I can still remember the first time the Peteks had my family over for supper and how good everything tasted and what fun we had.

When I began having ideas for this cookbook, I thought that I should remember my camera and take pictures of that tiny, but great house. In the fall of 2009, I finally remembered my camera. As I walked down First Avenue toward the house, I saw a backhoe in the yard and yellow tape wrapped around the trees. When I got there, the house was totally gone. Someone had demolished it and put it into a pile to be hauled away. I began to cry as I looked at the site of the destruction and devastation of June's last home in Lincoln. It was so sad to know that June had just died the year before and now the only reminder of her gracious presence in Lincoln, fifty years earlier, was also gone. As cute as that little house was, I couldn't think why someone wouldn't have had the foresight to use it for an entryway, den and upstairs guest bedroom. They could have then mashed the double-wide mobile home that was now in place, up against it, and give the new home some originality. I suppose it would have been an awful lot of work to pull something like that off.

So now as God holds June with Him in Heaven, I still hold her memories in my heart and hope to be able to share some of them with others.

Christmas was June's time to shine, as she went all out with decorating, as only she could do. Dorothy Anderson can still recall the details of how June used to decorate the Community Hall and banquet tables for the dinners and local festivities around the holidays. She still remembers the impact that June's presence left on our community. June had a talent for combining her gifts as a gracious hostess with elegant decorations and fantastic food. What a privilege to have had her in our midst for such a short time.

cozy

Pumpkin Walnut Cheesecake

Crust:

2 cups graham cracker crumbs **¼ cup sugar** **6 Tbsp. butter, melted**

Place a greased 9-inch springform pan on a double thickness of heavy-duty foil (about 18 inches square). Securely wrap foil around pan. In a small bowl combine cracker crumbs and sugar; stir in butter. Press onto the bottom and 1 inch up the sides of prepared pan.

Filling:

3 packages (8 oz. each) cream cheese, softened
¾ cup sugar
¾ cup brown sugar, packed
1 can (15 oz) solid-pack pumpkin
¼ cup heavy whipping cream
1 tsp. ground cinnamon
1 tsp. ground cloves
5 eggs, lightly beaten

In a large bowl, beat cream cheese and sugars until smooth. Beat in the pumpkin, cream, cinnamon and cloves until blended. Add eggs; beat on low speed just until they combine. Pour over crust. Place springform pan in a large baking pan; add 1 inch of hot water to larger pan. Bake at 325 degrees for 1 hour.

Topping:

6 Tbsp. butter, soft **1 cup brown sugar** **1 cup chopped walnuts**

Combine butter and brown sugar in a small bowl. Stir in walnuts. Carefully sprinkle over hot cheesecake. Bake 30 minutes longer or until center is just set. Remove springform pan from water bath. Cool on a wire rack for 10 minutes. Carefully run a knife around edge of pan to loosen. Cool 1 hour longer. Refrigerate overnight.

Chocolate Almond Silk Pie

Pie shell:

⅔ cup flour
2 Tbsp. powdered sugar
¼ cup butter
⅛ tsp. vanilla extract
3 Tbsp. chopped almonds, toasted

Combine first five ingredients in a small bowl. Beat on low speed until well combined, about 2-3 minutes. Press into the bottom and up the sides of a greased 9-inch pie plate. Bake at 400 degrees for 8 to 10 minutes or until golden. Cool on a wire rack.

Filling:

¾ cup sugar
3 eggs
3 squares (1 oz. each) unsweetened chocolate, coarsely chopped
⅛ tsp. almond extract
½ cup butter, softened
Sweetened whipped cream
Toasted sliced almonds

Combine sugar and eggs in a small sauce pan until well blended. Cook over low heat, stirring constantly until mixture reaches 160 degrees. Stir in unsweetened chocolate and almond extract until smooth. Cool to lukewarm stirring occasionally. In a large bowl, cream butter until light and fluffy. Add the cooled egg mixture; beat on high speed for 5 minutes. Pour into cooled pie shell. Cool for at least 6 hours before serving. Garnish with the whipped cream and almonds if desired.

I have just one more memory to share of June in her little home. Once when we were there for a Girl Scout meeting, one of the girls started banging on the piano, you know, the old chopstick number. I hadn't noticed a piano at the Peteks' home before, so I asked Connie who played the piano. Connie said her mother played a little bit. June could play whatever we asked her to because she could play by ear as well as read notes. We had a grand time singing songs with her accompanying us.

I have already told a out how June helped to orchestrate our 1955 Christmas program with Mrs. Donaldson. I never remembered who accompanied us on the piano then. There were several women who were good piano players back then. With June's musical talent and organizational skills, she certainly could have handled the job.

I did find this most amazing article published in the Lincoln paper, the *Blackfoot Valley Dispatch,* from March 19, 2009.

From out of the Past....

The Helena Independent Record printed a group of articles in April. 1949 highlighting Lincoln, its pioneer spirit and local lore, leading up to a 49er's dance. The following is another in a series of articles from yesteryear. The names mentioned in the article were a "who's who" of Lincoln society sixty years ago. The Helena Independent Record April 17, 1949 by C.J. Hansen

A gala evening is in store for everyone who attends the big 49er's dance and party at the Lincoln Community Hall Saturday night. "The main thing is to have a good time," said Don Roos, president of Lincolns' Community Association. "We try and make the celebration something to look forward to and something to remember." A promising floor show has been arranged complete with can-can girls. A barber shop quartet, a novelty act by Mr. and Mrs. Al Stoner and a Belle of the Ball skit by June Petek have also been arranged. Girls dancing in the chorus are Betty Hahn, Charlotte Smith, Ellen Lambkin, Evelyn Didriksen, Mary Hopkins and Irma Kary.

June Petek, Ellen Mulcare, Evelyn Didriksen and Mary Hopkins as "Can-can" dancers

Anybody ever wonder what happened to June Petek's piano? In 1959, June donated her piano to the newly constructed Methodist Church prior to moving.

Butterscotch Cheesecake

Crust:

1½ cups graham cracker crumbs **⅓ cup brown sugar** **⅓ cup butter, melted**

Place a greased 9-inch springform pan on a double thickness of heavy-duty foil (about 18 inches square). Securely wrap foil around pan. In a small bowl, combine the cracker crumbs and sugar; stir in butter. Press onto the bottom of prepared pan. Place pan on a baking sheet. Bake at 325 degrees for 10 minutes. Cool on a wire rack.

Filling:

1 can (14 oz.) sweetened condensed milk
1 package (3.4 oz.) instant butterscotch pudding mix
3 packages (8 oz. each) cream cheese, softened
¾ cup cold milk
1 tsp. vanilla extract
3 eggs, lightly beaten

In a small bowl, whisk the milks and pudding mix for 2 minutes. Let stand for 2 minutes or until soft-set. Meanwhile in a large bowl, beat cream cheese until smooth. Beat in pudding and vanilla. Add eggs; beat on low speed just until combined. Pour over crust. Place springform pan in a large baking pan; add 1 inch of hot water to larger pan. Bake at 325 degrees for 65 to 75 minutes or until center is almost set and top appears dull. Remove springform pan from water bath. Cool on a wire rack for 10 minutes. Carefully run a knife around edge of pan to loosen, cool 1 hour longer. Refrigerate overnight. Garnish with butterscotch topping and whipped cream if desired.

Frozen Cherry Dessert

Dorothy Andersons' *"Memories of Mom" Cookbook*

½ pound vanilla wafers
1 can Eagle Brand milk
1 (16 oz.) can crushed pineapple, drained
1 can cherry pie filling
½ tsp. vanilla extract
A few drops red food coloring
1 large container Cool Whip

my favorite recipe!

Crush vanilla wafers. Use ½ of wafers to line the bottom of a 9 x 11-inch cake pan. Combine milk, pineapple, flavoring, coloring and cherry pie filling. When stirred together well, fold in Cool Whip. Pour mixture into pan and spread evenly. Top with remaining crushed wafers. Freeze until ready to serve then cut into squares. Top with **whipped cream and a cherry.** ***Note:*** This recipe can also be used as a salad. Just ditch the wafers, chill instead of freezing and add **bananas and marshmallows** to the mixture just before serving.

Hershey Bar Dessert or Pie

(a variation of Vernie Burns' recipe from *The Old Lincoln Cookbook*)

16 large marshmallows
4 (1.5 oz.) Hershey bars (almonds or plain)
1 tsp. unflavored gelatin
½ cup cold milk
1 Tbsp. cold water
1 cup whipping cream

Melt marshmallows in milk in a double boiler. Add Hershey bars and melt. Soften gelatin in cold water. Add to Hershey mix. Cool before adding the whipped cream. Pour into graham cracker crust or use plain graham crackers crumbs for the bottom and the top. Chill.

In the midst of all the childhood fun and parties, there was heartache on First Avenue in 1959. It seemed that the Peteks had no more than moved into our neighborhood when they announced that they were moving away. Not to a neighboring city within the state or even a nearby state. The Peteks were moving to Alaska, a place that wasn't even a state yet. The whole community was so upset by their decision to leave Montana. They were leaving friends, family and Lincoln to go to a new frontier. Alaska was gaining lots of attention as a new promised land for adventurous people who wanted to make a new start. Every type of worker was needed to help get this new territory off the ground and toward statehood. There were rumors of how great the earnings would be for those who were ambitious enough to join the ranks of workers needed to establish businesses and homes.

Johnny Petek, who always reminded me of John Wayne, was a very generous and easy-going man. When he ran Stoner's Store, he extended credit for groceries, propane and gas with a trust that he would be paid by the end of the month in order to keep his business going. After closing the store, he continued extending credit to his propane customers. As time went by, he finally found himself in serious financial trouble.

As the story goes, he couldn't collect from some of his customers and got behind with his creditors. I remember a figure of $18,000 is what he owed when he couldn't collect from his non-paying propane customers. Now that was a lot of money back then. Just do the math: If a house worth $9,000 back then is now worth over $150,000, then $18,000 would be about equal to $300,000 now. Instead of filing for bankruptcy, his plan was to move to Alaska where things were happening and the money was good, and to get his debts paid down as fast as he could. He said he wouldn't return to the Lower 48 until all his creditors were paid in full. And he kept his word. Within three years, he paid off all his outstanding bills in Montana and was back on his feet in Alaska, running a successful business again. We all hoped and prayed that they would return to Montana once he was caught up, but that wasn't the case. The Peteks were hooked on Alaska and stayed there for many, many years.

Cathie and her husband, Bud, moved to Philomath, Oregon, prior to Johns death. June moved there also after John died, where she lived until her death in 2008. Connie and her husband, Randy, stayed in Alaska until Randy retired in 2008. They moved to Oregon and were able to be with June before she passed away.

There were parties before the Peteks left, but they weren't as happy as all the other parties had been. We didn't know if we would ever see them again. But as the years passed, the Peteks came to the Lower 48 for vacations, family events, weddings, and to see friends and relatives. My sister, Donna, and I traveled to Alaska for Cathie's wedding, and my husband and I also traveled to Alaska for our thirtieth wedding anniversary.

One day in May 1990, while I was working in St. Peter's Hospital ICU, a nice looking lady came walking down the hall like she was lost. When I finally realized it was June Petek, I almost fell over. She had flown down from Alaska to visit her brother who was critically ill. She was able to attend a graduation party the next night for our daughter Lisa.

CRAB SNACKS

Donna Hammer, Grandma Yuhas June and Johnny Petek and Uncle Bud at Portage Glacier, Alaska

Crab Wonton Cups

32 wonton wrappers
1 pkg. (8 oz.) cream cheese, softened
½ cup heavy whipping cream
1 Tbsp. Dijon mustard
1 tsp. Worcestershire sauce
5 drops hot pepper sauce
¼ cup thinly sliced green onion
Cooking spray
1 egg
2 pouches (3.53 oz. each) premium crab meat, drained
¼ cup sweet red pepper, finely chopped
1 cup grated Parmesan cheese

1. Press wonton wrappers into miniature muffin cups coated with cooking spray. Spritz wrappers with cooking spray. Bake at 350 degrees for 8 to 9 minutes or until lightly browned.
2. Meanwhile, in a small mixing bowl, beat the cream cheese, cream, egg mustard, Worcestershire sauce and pepper sauce until smooth. Stir in the crab, green onions and red pepper; spoon into wonton cups. Sprinkle with Parmesan cheese.
3. Bake for 10-12 min. or until filling is heated through. Serve warm

Crab-meat Canapes

½ cup butter softened
1 (6 oz.) can crab meat
1 jar (5 oz.) Old English Cheese
2 Tbsp. mayonnaise
½ tsp. seasoning salt
½ tsp. garlic salt (if desired)
6 English muffins sliced in halves

Mix first 6 ingredients together and spread on thick English muffin halves. Cut into quarters. Freeze on cookie sheet for three hours. Store in plastic bag in freezer until ready to use. Broil until hot and bubbly. Will keep in freezer up to 2 months.

Johnny Petek with Alaskan King Crab, 1966

Crab Cake Stuffed Portobellos

6 large portobello mushrooms
¾ cup finely chopped sweet onion
1 pkg. (8 oz.) cream cheese
½ cup seasoned bread crumbs
2 Tbsp. olive oil, *divided*
1 egg
1 tsp. Seafood seasoning
½ cup plus 1 tsp. grated Parmesan cheese, *divided*
2 cans (6½ oz. each) crab meat, drained

Remove stems from mushrooms (discard or save for another use); set caps aside. In a small skillet, sauté onion in 1 tablespoon oil until tender. In a small mixing bowl, combine the cream cheese, egg, bread crumbs, ½ cup Parmesan cheese and seafood seasoning. Gently stir in crab.
Spoon ½ cup crab mixture into each mushroom cap; drizzle with remaining oil. Sprinkle with paprika and remaining Parmesan cheese. Place in a greased 10 x 15-inch baking pan. Bake, uncovered, at 400 degrees for 15 to 20 minutes or until mushrooms are tender.

Johnny Petek and Donna Alaska, 1966

One party that stands out in my memory is the "housewarming party" of 1960. This party took place in a brand new house my Dad built on the corner of First Avenue and B Street. Dad had bought three lots, one acre each, starting just one block from the main highway by Leeper's Motel. He bought the ground from Dee Leeper, who had built the motel and several cabins in the area sometime before we ever moved to Lincoln. Dee was the sheriff of Cascade County in Great Falls. Dad became acquainted with him through my uncle, Ubal Landry. Ubal was married to my Dad's sister, Helen. They lived in Belt, Montana, where Ubal served as under-sheriff during the 1940s and 1950s.

After Dad finished our house, he began to build this little house next door to ours. He started it as a spec house hoping to attract a buyer who would be able to supply some of the cash necessary to complete the job. Since a buyer didn't come forth as planned, he had to borrow money to complete the project. I can remember a discussion every month between my parents about the amount of money needed for the new house that was necessary for other things. My mother felt the little house was just a "pipe dream" of my dad's and that everybody was laughing at his silly idea for a spec house in Lincoln; thus it was labeled "Hammers Folly." My sister and I never felt that way and thought it was a great idea and a beautiful house.

While our parents were planning a little getaway for a weekend out of town, Donna and I were busy making plans for a little party in the new house when they left. We plotted with the girls from our classes to have a slumber party and combined dance class, so we would all know how to dance when we went off to Augusta to high school.

Claudia Wildin, and Terry Routzahn had begun to teach us how to dance before they went off to high school. They told us we would need to know the art of dancing, especially the jitterbug, as the Augusta boys were pretty good dancers. We had good music back then with many great artists like Elvis, the Beach Boys, Johnny Cash, plus our own hometown artist, Jimmy Schaffer.

Pop Corn Balls Karla Anderson Butcher

6 to 8 cups popped corn
1 cup light corn syrup
2 cups sugar
½ cup water
½ tsp. soda
1 Tbsp. butter
1 tsp. vanilla extract
Food coloring of choice

Keep popcorn hot and crisp in slow oven (200 degrees). Cook sugar, water and corn syrup to very hardball stage (265 degrees). Remove from heat and add soda, butter and vanilla and coloring. Pour slowly over popped corn in a very large bowl, stirring all the while, until all kernels are coated. Form into balls. Use butter on hands if necessary.

Salted Nut Rolls Lana Anderson Moyer

1 can sweetened condensed milk
1 package of peanut butter chips
2 Tbsp. of margarine or butter
1 (16 oz.) jar of salted roasted peanuts
4 cups of miniature marshmallows

In a large bowl, mix peanut butter chips, butter or margarine, and sweetened condensed milk. Microwave on high for 2 minutes (stir it one minute) or until melted.

Butter a 9 x 13-inch pan; pour half of the peanuts into pan. Add marshmallows to melted mixture until well coated. Pour melted mixture over peanuts; spread. Pour rest of peanuts over top of mixture and press down into melted mixture.

Homemade Caramel Corn Lisa Anderson Hammel

20 cups popped popcorn
½ cup dark corn syrup
1 cup mixed salted nuts
2 cups packed brown sugar
½ tsp. salt
1 cup butter
½ tsp. soda

Heat oven to 200 degrees. Place popped corn in a roasting pan. In a 2 quart pan, mix brown sugar, butter, corn syrup and salt. Cook over medium heat until full boil (12 to 14 minutes). Continue cooking until 238 degrees. Remove from heat, stir in soda. Pour over popcorn; sprinkle nuts over caramel. Stir until all popcorn is coated. Bake 20 minutes. Stir and bake 25 minutes more. Place on waxed paper; let cool. Break into pieces and store in airtight containers.

Heath Bars Greta Koss Buehler

40 soda crackers
1 cup butter
1 cup brown sugar
1 (12 oz. pkg.) milk chocolate chips
1 cup chopped nuts

Place crackers on cookie sheet with an edge (11x16-inch). Boil sugar and butter 2 to 3 minutes. Pour sugar mixture over crackers. Place in a 350 degree oven for 5 minutes or until crackers float. Pour chocolate chips on top and spread when melted. Sprinkle with chopped walnuts. Cut in squares.

Chicken Dinner Bars Kerry Koss Bystrom

½ cup butter
32 large marshmallows
8 cups rice Krispies
1½ cups white Karo syrup
1 cup sugar
1½ cups peanut butter
Topping of choice such as M&M's or Chocolate chips

Melt butter and marshmallows in large pan. Remove from heat. Stir in Rice Krispies. Spread in greased cookie sheet. Bring sugar and Karo syrup to a boil. Remove from heat. Add peanut butter and stir. Pour on top of Rice Krispies. Sprinkle on topping of choice and cool.

Sweets and Treats - above recipes by granddaughters of Don Hammer

The house with its large living room and new plywood flooring was the ideal place for an all-night-dance and slumber party. So all the girls from the seventh and eighth grade classes waited in secret until Mom and Dad left town. Since the house had heat and plumbing already in place, it couldn't be more perfect. We all danced every type of dance we would need to know to make it to the big time, a school dance at Augusta High School. I don't think we slept much in our sleeping bags as we danced and giggled most of the night. We all brought treats and snacks and records and had a wonderful time. No phones, texting, parents, boys, booze or drugs to worry about. Just a bunch of Lincoln girls having an old-fashioned good time. Our neighbors, the Quilters, who were looking after us for the weekend, somehow seemed to know about this party and our plans, as probably did all the parents whose kids were there also.

Bob and Deanne Moffitt

The house sold soon after that to the Moffitts from Chester, Mt. Bob Moffitt was a retired farmer who bought the house and about 400 acres of land west of Lincoln, from the edge of town up to the Beaver Creek Road. Bob ran cattle there until he was too old to care for them. He leased out the ground after that. Bob and Deanne Moffitt sort of adopted our family after our dad's death and gave us a second home to return to in Lincoln after my mother sold our home to Bob Moffitt's son from California. The Moffitt's said they bought that house for about $7,000 back in1960 with Dad only charging enough to pay off his creditors and for the supplies he purchased with his own capital. After they bought the house, they hired him to add on a sun porch on the back with windows all around and a covered patio.

The Moffitt's lived in that little house until their deaths. Bob died in 1995 and Deanne in 2005. They had agreed to leave the house to my sister and I since we would appreciate the sentimental value of it. They also felt they had gotten the house at a steal since Dad was so desperate to get rid of it that he never charged near what it was actually worth. Inheriting that house was such a blessing to us since it was one of the last homes in Lincoln that Dad built before his death. Of course there are drawbacks to inheriting a house. As any homeowner knows, the taxes, insurance, utilities, upkeep and repairs can get quite expensive. My sister, with her practical side, felt it should be sold as soon as we had it cleaned out and the necessary repairs and painting done. With all my dreams and memories, I felt someone should keep it as a possible retirement home. So the only solution seemed that my husband and I should buy my sister's share and complete some updating projects so that we could later retire there.

One day, I got a phone call from a lady I did not know, inquiring about renting our little house on the corner of First Avenue and B Street. She said she had walked by it many, many times and it looked so forlorn and lonely with no one living there. She said she would love to rent it and spend her retirement years there. I got glowing references for her from mutual friends, Carla Anderson, the McClures and Pauline Orr. Everyone else who knew Nellie Knight also told me what a wonderful Christian lady she was and how she would take such good care of our home.

It is amazing to see how God takes care of his own children. Nellie needed a comfortable home to spend her retirement years in. I needed someone to live in the house and take care of the last gift from my earthly father via the Moffitts. What a joy to have her as a new friend that connects the past with the present. What a joy also to know that our relationship with our heavenly father will assure us of our shared goal—spending eternity together in His presence when we are done enjoying our time here on this earth and in Lincoln, Montana. I don't know how it can get much better than that, but they say it will be unbelievable and far more beautiful than we can ever imagine.

So once again there is life, love and laughter (I don't know about dancing) on First Avenue.

Daddy's Chocolate Cake

Deanne Moffitt
Lincoln Cookbook

2½ cups flour, sifted
1½ cup sugar
2 tsp. baking soda
1 tsp. salt
4 Tbsp. cocoa
⅔ cup shortening, soft
2 eggs
1 cup buttermilk
½ cup water
1 tsp. vanilla extract

Sift flour, sugar, cocoa, baking soda, salt into bowl. Add shortening, eggs, buttermilk, water and vanilla extract. Beat at medium speed for 3 minutes until batter is smooth. Pour into greased 9 x 13-inch pan. Bake at 350 degrees for 35-40 minutes.

Old Fashioned Fruitcake

A family recipe of Deanne Moffitt

1 pound raisins (3 cups)
1 pound currents
1 box of red cherries
1 box of green cherries
1 bottle maraschino cherries plus juice
1 pound dates
1 box mixed fruit or other fruit such as citron, apricots, figs or pineapple.

Bring fruit to a boil or get hot stirring with 2½ cups water and cherry juice. Soak fruit in liquid overnight, covered with tin foil. If any liquid remains on the fruit in the morning, drain it off or the dough will be to thin. *(Deanne may have used a little brandy in the liquid when soaking the fruit)*

Cake Batter -- Cream together:

¾ cup butter
1 cup brown sugar
1 cup white sugar
4 eggs (add 1 egg at a time and beat well after each egg is added)
1 cup molasses

Sift together and add to creamed mixture alternately with **½ cup buttermilk:**

4 cups flour
1 tsp. cinnamon
1 tsp. cloves
1 tsp. allspice
1 tsp. nutmeg
1 tsp. salt
1 tsp. baking soda

add: **½ to 1 cup chopped pecans or walnuts** to batter

Prepare baking pans such as bread pans, or long loaf type angel food cake pan. Line pans with brown paper or grocery sacks cut to fit. Then line with waxed paper, greased with butter, oil or cooking spray. Fill pans about 2/3 full of batter. May also place a pan with water on the bottom shelf of oven for moisture. Bake in a 250 to 275 degree oven for 4 to 5 hours, depending on the size of the pans. Test in 4 to 5 hours with a toothpick for doneness.

Chex Muddy Buddies

Carla Anderson
Lincoln School Cookbook

9 cups your favorite Chex brand cereal-- (Corn, Rice, Wheat, Double multi-bran or Frosted Rice Chex Jrs.)
1½ cups powdered sugar
1 cup semi-sweet chocolate chips
½ cup peanut butter
¼ cup margarine or butter
¼ tsp. vanilla extract

Pour cereal into a large bowl. Combine chips, peanut butter and margarine in a 1 quart microwave safe bowl. Heat on high 1 to 1½ minutes or until smooth, stirring after 1 minute. Stir in vanilla. Pour chocolate mixture over cereal, stirring until all pieces are evenly coated. Pour cereal mixture into a plastic bag with powdered sugar. Seal securely. Shake until all pieces are well coated. Spread on wax paper to cool. Store in resealable plastic bags or airtight container.

See pages 55 and 99 for recipes by Nellie Knight and her daughter-in-law Peggy Knight

As I close this section of the cookbook, I realize that I have not included the recipes for my favorite birthday cakes. These are the cakes I have made over the years for my own daughters and nieces. The banana split cake recipe came from the *Lincoln Cookbook (1977),* and the banana custard chiffon cake recipe came from *The Country Fair Cookbook (1975),* written by the food editors of the *Farm Journal* magazine. Both of those cookbooks were gifts from Deanne Moffit when they came out in print. I have just about worn the covers off both cookbooks since I use them so much. Deanne Moffit gave the same cookbooks to my sister, but she has taken better care of hers. Donna has a system of making a scrapbook for her favorite recipes, that also includes pictures of those that she cuts out of magazines.

I started out this section describing birthday parties that June Petek and Juna McClure gave for their children. I have tried to pass that tradition down with my own daughters as they now do for their children. Birthday parties are a special way of showing our love for our families, especially the children. The party and the planner will be remembered much longer than any of the gifts.

Karla Anderson in 1977 on her eighth birthday with a banana split cake

Karla in 1992, age 23, with a Garfield theme birthday party

Lisa Anderson age 18, 1990

Karla, Lisa and Lana with cousins Greta and Kerry Koss in 1979. Kerry, four years old, with her Holly Hobby cake.

Lana Anderson, age 19, 1996

Kerry and Donna Koss on Kerry's tenth birthday, 1985

Happy Birthday

Banana Custard Chiffon Cake

2¼ cups sifted cake flour
1½ cups sugar
3 tsp. baking powder
1 tsp. salt
½ cup cooking oil
5 egg yolks
¾ cup mashed bananas (2 medium)
1 Tbsp. lemon juice
1 tsp. vanilla extract
1 cup egg whites (7 or 8)
½ tsp. cream of tartar

Sift together cake flour, sugar, baking powder and salt into bowl. Make a well in the center; add oil, egg yolks, bananas, lemon juice and vanilla. Beat with electric mixer at low speed 1 minute. Beat egg whites and cream of tartar until stiff peaks form. Gradually pour egg yolk mixture over whites, folding just until blended. Pour batter into ungreased 10-inch tube pan. Cut through batter with spatula. Bake in 325 degrees oven 50 to 60 minutes or until cake tests done. Invert tube pan on funnel or bottle to cool. When completely cooled, remove from pan.

Happy Birthday

Banana Split Cake

Lincoln Cookbook

Crust: **2 cups crushed graham crackers** **⅓ cup sugar** **5 Tbsp. melted butter**

Pat crust into a 9 x 13-inch pan. Bake 8 to 9 minutes at 350 degrees. Cool.

Filling: **2 cups powdered sugar** **2 sticks butter** **1 tsp. vanilla extract**
2 whole eggs (May want to nuke them) Cream together and spread carefully over crumbs.

Topping: **4-5 bananas** **1 large can pineapple, crushed plus 1 small can**
2 boxes frozen sliced strawberries or fresh strawberries (opt.)
Cool Whip **Nuts (chopped)** **Maraschino cherries, chopped, drained (opt)**

Slice the bananas lengthwise and layer over the creamed filling; drain the pineapple and spread it over the bananas. Place strawberries on top of pineapple if using them. Spread the top with Cool Whip and sprinkle chopped nuts over all. Sprinkle cherries over the top if desired. Cover with foil and chill at least 6 hours or overnight.

Banana Cake

Maxine Roos
Lincoln Cookbook

1¼ cup brown sugar
½ cup shortening
2 eggs
2 cups flour
1 tsp. baking powder
½ tsp. salt
1 tsp. soda
1 cup sour cream
1 tsp. vanilla extract
2 bananas, mashed

Mix as you would any cake, adding bananas last. Bake a loaf cake at 375 degrees for 45 minutes, cake pan for 30 minutes. Very ripe, soft bananas make the best flavored cake.

Banana Pudding Dessert

1½ cups water
1 pkg. (6 oz.) vanilla pudding mix
1 (14 oz.) can sweetened condensed milk
1 box vanilla wafers
3 cups heavy cream
4 bananas, sliced

Blend the water, pudding mix and condensed milk until well mixed. Refrigerate at least 4 hours or overnight. Whip the heavy cream until soft peaks form. Fold the pudding mixture into the whipped cream until well incorporated. In a trifle bowl, layer wafers, sliced bananas then pudding mixture. Continue until all of the mixture is used ending with the pudding mixture. Refrigerate 30 minutes.

Penuche Icing

½ cup margarine: Melt in sauce pan
Add: **1 cup brown sugar** and boil over low heat 2 minutes, stirring constantly. Stir in **¼ cup milk** and bring to a boil, cool. Add: **2 cups powdered sugar.**

Banana Cake

Lisa Anderson, nine years old, in 1981

Birthday parties for Greta Koss, Donna's daughter

Evelyn Hammer Young's 90th birthday party in 2011

Four year old Lisa Anderson with sister, Karla in 1976

A cousin celebration of birthdays for Lana Anderson and Greta Koss with Kerry Koss and Lisa Anderson helping them open their gifts.

These last few pages of birthday parties are of the granddaughters of Donald and Evelyn Hammer.

Birthday parties were not the only form of entertainment in our little backwoods town. Saturday nights always brought forth some form of interesting activities and adventures. Along with live music and dancing at the local bars, there was the occasional community dances at the Community Hall. But for our family, Saturday nights usually consisted of watching TV gathered around our warm woodstove. The lineup of TV favorites were *the Lawrence Welk Show, the Red Skeleton Hour, The Dean Martin Variety Show* and the evening's grand finale of *Gunsmoke*.

Donna and I would whip up a batch of our ever popular fudge, divinity, taffy or popcorn. We would try to make popcorn balls but always seemed to burn the syrup, as it took forever for that stuff to reach the right temperature. Nobody had the patience to stand there and wait for that to happen. That burned sugary substance made a smell that lingered around the house for days, and cleanup of the pan was impossible.

On one occasion there was a boxing match scheduled for a Saturday night. Right before the event of the century was to take place, the electricity went out. This was a common occurrence back then, and we had lanterns, candles and wood heat and could make do with games, piano music or a walk outdoors while waiting for the electricity to return. Dad had no patience for a blackout that evening and was determined to watch that boxing match. He had a portable generator (light plant) in his shop from which he ran a long extension cord into the house to plug the TV into. In the back of my mind I didn't figure a fight was worth all the effort, and my mother was verbally warning him about the bad things that could happen with such a stunt. He paid no attention to her warnings and was bound and determined to fire up that TV, and that is just what he did. He blew up that big old expensive picture tube, and we spent the rest of that winter without a TV.

We still found ways to have fun without a TV. There would be "jam sessions" where some of the local musicians would gather with guitars and mother would play the piano. There were the wild nighttime toboggan rides. My favorite, though, was the board games of Monopoly and Scrabble. Dad was actually quite good at those games and I soon learned the art of winning at Monopoly. Dad taught us to take a risk by borrowing or mortgaging our game board properties in order to build up our better properties to make more income. The secret then became to sit it out in jail and collect rent off the expensive properties and ultimately be the winner. Those games took awhile and usually had to be paused and resumed the next day. Dad and I would always beat Mom and Donna out early on as they saw the foolishness of the game and found more useful things to do. In fact, I loved that game so much that I would take "sick days" from school and play Monopoly all alone while "sick" in bed. I would pretend to be two different people. By devising a split personality approach, one of my people would be the winner and the other the loser, and the competition between the two could become quite incredible. Sometimes it took a little maneuvering (cheating) to make sure my predetermined winner personality won the game.

Karleen and Andy Anderson

After going off to high school in Augusta, Saturday nights took on a new flavor. Boys from Augusta would drive up to Lincoln and then go to Lincoln girls' homes to see if the girl could go out for an evening of cruising and nonsense. The boys were readily accepted at some homes, but not so at our home. It took an extremely brave and bold type of a fellow to come into our home and ask our dad if we could go out for the evening.

Donald Hammer

Dad had a thing he did with the newspaper that gave the signal whether it was OK to ask for permission or not. If he put his news paper down and allowed an introduction, then it was OK to ask his permission. If the newspaper stayed up, it meant "No way, so don't even ask." The fellow would then bid his adios and head to the home of some other girl with more congenial parents.

When Donna and I started to work as waitresses during the summer of our later high school years, our dad gave us a stern warning about dating strangers. He told us that if a stranger should ask us out on a date and wouldn't take a simple "No" for an answer but asked us why we wouldn't go with him, then we were to just say that "my dad won't let me date strangers."

Looking back, that plan was possibly the beginning of the end for our dad. Not until Donna and I were painting in the Moffit home some forty years after our dad died, did we ever discuss Dad and his rules. Up until that time, we had never told anyone, not even each other, that Charles Corliss, the man who murdered our Dad, had asked each of us out on a date when he approached us at our respective places of employment. As we had been instructed, we both answered his" why" question with the same reply about our dad not allowing us to date strangers. Just two days later, our dad was missing and the horrible reality began. He was gone forever and taken away when his young family and a growing community needed him. He was taken during the best time of his young life while living out his dreams in Lincoln, Montana.

Living with that guilt all those years about the possibility that our saying "No" to a psychopathic killer and putting the blame on our dad has been a bit much for both Donna and I to handle. We will never know the reason Corliss chose our dad as his victim, but the passing years have taught us that God is in control, and that He has a reason and a master plan for our lives that we will only understand when we meet Him at the gates of Heaven.

I will share more of my thoughts on this subject in the next volume of this book, which is currently being written for release in the near future.

After looking back over this incident in my life, my fear of ever dating someone I didn't know meant that the dating years were over. After Dad's death, I figured I had better only date the fellow that my dad had put his newspaper down for and was interested in meeting and getting to know.

The photo below reminds me of a swampy area along Highway 200 between Lincoln and Rogers Pass. This is probably the way it looked that final day as my dad was taken up the road toward the pass knowing he would never be back that way again.

Marshlands by Gus Wolfe

The previous pages of birthday parties were of Donald Hammer's grandchildren and wife, Evelyn. He was never able to meet or enjoy any family times with the granddaughters, who are Karla, Lisa and Lana Anderson and Greta and Kerry Koss. He would have certainly enjoyed all the parties with all seventeen of his great grandchildren as well. He has been greatly missed these last 50 years.

Above picture of Donald Hammer preparing to hook up a toboggan to his truck filled with excited kids. The kids are cousins Walter and Charlotte Mehmke and Donna and Karleen Hammer. Picture taken by Uncle Carl Mehmke before 1960.

I don't want to leave this story about growing up in Lincoln on a negative note. Everyone has tradgedy and heartache in their lifetime. Those are the times that help us to appreciate the good times and the "good old days" that were filled with parties, fun, adventures and great memories.

So in conclusion, anytime can be partytime when growing up in Lincoln, Montana. It didn't have to be just for birthday parties or programs at the Lincoln School or the Community Hall that we would celebrate. Any winter outdoor activity would turn into a party when we would go to someone's home to warm up after our big adventure and have fun, laughter and lots of

When I Look Back at Lincoln, Montana

When I looked back, I remember seeing you wearing the apron that I sewed for you, and I then wanted to sew more difficult projects.

When I looked back, I remember seeing you feed a stray cat, and I learned that it was good to be kind to animals.

When I looked back, I remember seeing you make a birthday party into a memorable event for me and my friends, along with all the cool treats and a favorite cake. I learned that the little things can be the special things.

When I looked back, I remember hearing you say a prayer, and I knew that there is a God I could always talk to, and I learned to trust in Him.

When I looked back, I remember seeing you make a meal and take it out to the men working in the fields, and I saw how much they appreciated your efforts. Preparing a meal is a way to show our concern for others and a way to help care for each other.

When I looked back, I remember seeing how much fun you had with children when helping them to ice-skate or pulling the toboggan and sleds in the new snow. I learned to appreciate the adults who took the time to play with us and care for us.

When I looked back, I remember seeing how you handled your responsibilities and put all your efforts into any job, from building quality homes for friends or family, to peeling logs for building cabins and lodges. I learned that I would also have to be responsible when I grow up.

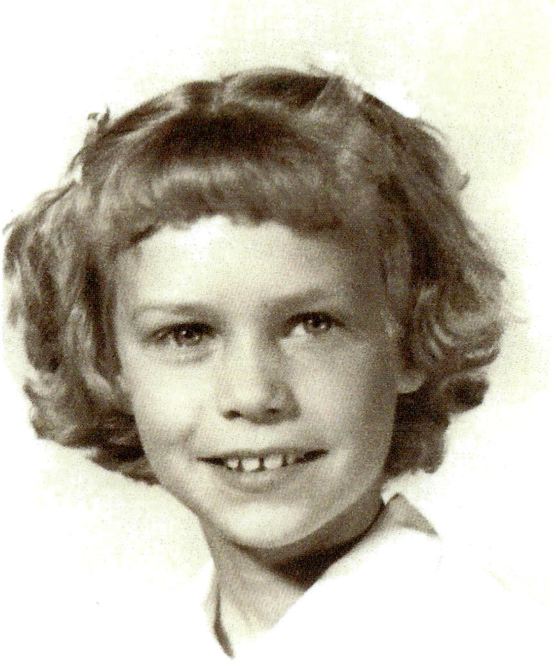

When I looked back, I remember seeing tears come from your eyes, and I learned that sometimes things hurt, but it's all right to cry.

When I looked back, I remembered how a whole community came together to stand by a family in a time of crisis. It showed that they cared, and I wanted to be able to help others like that someday.

When I looked back, I remembered you and wanted to say, "Thanks for all the things I remembered when I was looking back at Lincoln, Montana."

INDEX

CANDIES

COOKIES

COOKIES—BARS and SQUARES

CHEESECAKES

DESSERTS

EGGS AND BRUNCH

ENTREES

Chicken

Frankfurters

FROSTINGS

PIES, Pastries and Pasties

MISCELLANEOUS

SALADS

SANDWICHES

TREATS

Acknowledgments

I want to thank many people who helped me get this book off the ground. There were those who provided family photos, others with their talent for artwork such as painting, drawing, needlework and photography. Thanks for giving your permission to use your artwork along with stories and remembrances of your Lincoln parents, families and homes. Thanks also to those people for allowing me to use family stories as I remember them. I have portrayed most of the Lincoln people that I grew up with as heroes, and they are in my opinion. You no longer see the kind of small town devotion of the older generation to the children as what I saw when I was growing up.

Thanks again for allowing me to use the artwork of the artists and friends listed below that help to portray the essence of growing up in Lincoln, Montana with its special people and places.

My special thanks to Kathy Springmeyer and Shirley Machonis of Farcountry Press and Sweetgrass Books for their encouragement, guidance and editing skills. They were so patient as they helped me clean up my original mess.

Alden, Mary; *Cookbook for Children* (1956), p. 20

American Greeting Corporation permission to use cards on pp. 70, 114, and 116

Augusta High School Annual *The Wapiti* (1963) p. 64, (1965) pp. 46 and 153

Baril, Nina; oil paintings of: *The Lincoln Community Hall*, p. 102; *The Bridge Over the Blackfoot*, p. 10; and *Lambkins' Bar and Café*, p. 7

Barrett, Jackie; photograph of Steamboat Mountain at Augusta, MT, p. 53

Better Homes and Gardens Jr. Cookbook for the Hostess and Host of Tomorrow (1955), pp.15 and 55

Betty Crocker's Picture Cookbook (1950), First Edition, pp. 12, 44, and 84

Betty Crocker's Cooky Book (1963), pp. 82, 84, and 99

Blackfoot Valley Dispatch articles, pp. 68, 76, 79, and 136

Burns, Jerry; drawing for *The Lincoln Cookbook*, p. 18

Butcher grandchildren pictures, p. 107

Cozzolino, Sandra "Winter Season" Cross Stitch chart is used with permission of Sandra Cozzilino and is available by contacting Imaginating at www.imaginating.com

Ellingsen, John D.; *The Mehmke's gave a Party* (1966), p. 123

Gold Pans and Singletrees (1994), Lincoln History Book

Great Falls Tribune (2007) article by Kim Skornogoski, p. 60

Hammel grandchildren, pp. 43 and 106

Hammer, Evelyn; home photos, pp. 54 and 134

Howard, James; watercolor, *Race to the Sky* (2010), p. 80

Johnson, Judy; oil painting, *Race to the Sky* (2012), p. 81

Koss, Donna Hammer; paintings and drawings of *Stoner's Store*, p. 14; *Matt King Home*, p. 22; *piano*, p. 26; *chickadee*, p. 35; and *cabins*, pp. 90 and 132

Kay, Sarah; "Holly Hobby" drawings from internet public domain sites, pp. 119, 124, 125, 128, 130, and 140

Lincoln School Annual *The Evergreen*, (1956), pp. 84, 86, 88, 90, 92, 94, 96, 98, and 100

Lincoln School photos, pp. 94 and 154

Mains, Karen; *Open Heart, Open Home: The Hospitable Way to Make Others Feel Welcome & Wanted*, (1997), IntraVarsity Press, www.ivpress.com, pp. 69 and 79

McClure, Bob; family photographs, pp. 62, 64 and 66

Mehmke, Charlotte; photos of Mehkme Steam Engines and family, pp. 122, 123, and 153

Morgan, Bob; oil painting of *Historic Lincoln*, p. 38

Moyer, Lana and family, pp. 32 and 106

Petek, Cathie and Connie; family photos, pp. 14, 16, 41, 56, 116, and 118

Petek, June; drawings, *Party Lady*, p. 13; *Stoner's Store*, p. 14; *Lambkins*, p. 39; card, p. 40; *Santa* p. 82 and 111; *School House*, p. 90; *Community Hall*, pp. 92 and 102.

Orr, Bob; family photo, p. 76

Shaw, Joyce; photos, pp. 44 and 48

Snowmen from copyright free internet sites, pp. 2, 51, 52, 54, 56, 69, 76, 77, 88, 93, 106, 113, 115, 133, 142, and 143

Stoney Creek Cross Stitch Designs, p. 44 and 53

Story of Lincoln 1860s-1989 photos, pp. 39, 103, and 140

Strope, Ellen; copyright free internet photo, p. 49

Vintage Christmas cards from public domain internet sites, pp. 69, 76, 51, 104, 105, 125, 126, and 139

Ward, Ann; family photos, p. 30

Wilton Cake Decorating Yearbook (1970), www.wilton.com, pp. 115, 117 and 119

Wolfe, Gus; photographs, pp. 48, 52, 78, 81, and 152